Speak, Read, Write Russian

Here is a method of learning to speak and read and write Russian naturally, taking grammar and vocabulary by easy stages. It is a basic book, and its object is to teach quickly. Anyone keen enough to study for a few hours every week should be able to master simple Russian, using words and phrases in everyday use, in a very short time.

The rules of grammar have been reduced to a minimum. To help you to cope with the Russian alphabet, phonetic transcriptions are given throughout, so that pronunciation presents no problems. The words and sentences given as grammatical examples are the kind you would need for everyday life in Russia, sightseeing, travelling, shopping, as a tourist or business visitor, enabling you to use this book as a phrase book as well as for study.

Other titles in this series

SPEAK, READ, WRITE FRENCH — Harry Baptist Smith
SPEAK, READ, WRITE GERMAN — Christine Sutton
SPEAK, READ, WRITE ITALIAN — J. M. Forsey
SPEAK, READ, WRITE SPANISH — R. T. Beckingham

Tandem editions 25p

This book is sold subject to the condition that it shall not, by way of trade, be lent, re-sold, hired out or otherwise disposed of without the publisher's consent, in any form of binding or cover other than that in which it is published.

Speak, Read, Write Russian

Y. B. Panferova

With additional material by
K. Taylor and F. Smitham

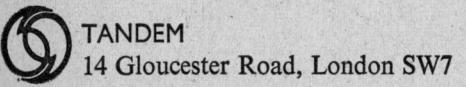
TANDEM
14 Gloucester Road, London SW7

First published in Great Britain by Universal-Tandem
Publishing Co. Ltd, 1972

Published in association with the Novosti Press Agency
Copyright © Universal-Tandem Publishing Co. Ltd, 1972

Printed in Great Britain by R. & R. Clark Ltd, Edinburgh

CONTENTS

Introduction	7
The alphabet	9
Let's go	10
Some useful phrases	12
Arrival, the hotel	16
A simple verb	21
To begin, v.	21
At	22
To be, v., Before	23
Bring, v.	25
Can, may, be able, v.	26
To ask permission, v.	27
Conjunctions	28
To eat, v.	29
Eating	30
Enquiries	33
To read, v.	39
To reply, answer, v.	40
To say, tell, speak, v.	41
To see, v.	43
Shopping	44
Sightseeing	47
Some—any	50
Tenses	51
Present Tense	51
To ask, to give, v.	52
To hurry, v.	54
Past Tense, Future Tense	55
Idioms	57
Expressions of time	58
Time by the clock	59
Verbs of movement	62
To go (verbs)	62
Travelling	67
To understand, v.	70
Days of the week	71
Months, seasons	72
Possession	73
To have	77
Health	79

Post Office, telephone	81
To want, wish, v.	84
The weather	85
The verb (contd.)	88
Subjunctive, Imperative	89
Gender of nouns	92
Plural of nouns	94
Adjectives	98
Use of short forms	100
Demonstratives	105
Adverbs	107
Age	110
To agree	111
Pronouns	112
Cases of Pronouns	113
Interrogatives	115
To invite, v.	117
To know, v.	118
To allow, let, v.	119
To live, stay, v.	120
Liquid refreshments	121
To like, love, prefer, v.	123
To make, to do	125
Cases of nouns	127
Every, everybody, everything	134
To feel, v.	135
Must, ought, should, v.	136
To need	137
Negation	138
Numerals	141
Ordinal numbers	143
One—They	145
To pay, v.	146
Meeting people	148
Money matters	151
Use of 'about'	152
Prepositions	153
In, into, to	157
The passive voice	158
To write, v.	159

INTRODUCTION

Russian is the mother tongue of a family of closely related Slavonic languages which includes Slovak, Czech, Polish, Yugoslav, Serbian and Bulgarian.

At first sight the characters of the alphabet may appear very strange. They date back to the 9th century A.D. Up to that time the Slavs had no written language at all.

In a book of this size it is possible merely briefly to sketch the background of the Slav peoples, who comprise the largest ethnic race in Europe.

Presumably they lived originally along the shores of the north-east rivers of the Carpathian Mountains. A great migration of ancient tribes took place in prehistoric times. By the first century A.D. one Slav tribe had already settled in Slovakia. Another tribe went further north. They were the forefathers of the Poles. Those who went south (in Russian 'Yug') became the Yugoslavs. By far the largest tribe continued eastwards. In the passage of time they became the Russians. Various groups among this tribe crossed the Ural Mountains and went on far into Siberia where they settled.

The two greatest powers in the world were the Greek Empire (Byzantium) and the Holy Roman Empire. Two monks, Kyril and Methodius, on instructions from the Greek government, designed an alphabet for the Slavs based on the Greek tongue. They then translated the most important prayers and liturgies into the new 'Slavonic' language and, thereby, gave the Slavs their own written language and at the same time introduced them to Christianity.

At some later period in their history the Western Slavs,

notably the Czechs and Poles, accepted the protection and authority of the Holy Roman Empire and 'Latinised' their alphabet in the process. The Russians chose Byzantium and, to this day, have kept their 'Kyrillic' alphabet.

The aim of this book is simply to provide a working knowledge of a rich and beautifully sounding language which, in our modern world, is a 'must' for every forward-thinking person.

The accent is on helping the visitor to Russia, whether a tourist on holiday or on a business trip; but the serious student or anybody studying languages as a pleasant hobby will also find much to interest him.

Russian is not really so difficult to learn. Since it is pronounced almost exactly as it is written it is virtually a phonetic language. So, to simplify matters, all the Russian words and phrases in this book are repeated phonetically in English. However when 'o' is the vowel of an unstressed syllable it is quite frequently pronounced as a shortened 'a', and so though the written vowel may be an 'o', sometimes in the phonetic transliteration 'a' is given.

Many words, of course, have more than one syllable and only one of them is stressed. There is no hard and fast rule, however, to indicate which syllable is stressed. This knowledge is gained in the gradual mastery of the language. In order to help you on your way the stressed syllable will be shown with this accent: '. It is important to get the correct stress, as an incorrect one can change the entire meaning of a word.

Now let us spend a little time getting used to the sight and sound of the Kyrillic characters.

THE ALPHABET

Printed		Written		English phonetic pronunciation
А	а	*А*	*а*	a as in 'car'
Б	б	*Б*	*б*	b as in 'best' and 'p' at the end of a word
В	в	*В*	*в*	v as in 'vine' and 'f' at the end of a word
Г	г	*Г*	*г*	g as in 'good' and 'k' at the end of a word
Д	д	*Д*	*дg*	d as in 'did' and 't' at the end of a word
Е	е	*Е*	*е*	ye as in 'yes'
Ё	ё	*Ё*	*ё*	yo as in 'yonder'
Ж	ж	*Ж*	*ж*	zh as in 'pleasure' and 'sh' at the end of a word
З	з	*З*	*зз*	z as in 'zoo'
И	и	*И*	*и*	i as in 'pit'
Й	й	*Й*	*й*	y as in 'joy'
К	к	*К*	*к*	k as in 'kiss'
Л	л	*Л*	*л*	l as in 'tall'
М	м	*М*	*м*	m as in 'map'
Н	н	*Н*	*н*	n as in 'nice'
О	о	*О*	*о*	o as in 'hop'
П	п	*П*	*п*	p as in 'pop'
Р	р	*Р*	*р*	r as in 'error' (with a distinct trill)
С	с	*С*	*с*	s as in 'set'
Т	т	*Т*	*т*	t as in 'time'
У	у	*У*	*у*	u as in 'put' or in 'sugar'
Ф	ф	*Ф*	*ф*	f as in 'fine'
Х	х	*Х*	*х*	kh as in 'loch' (Scottish)

Printed	Written	English phonetic pronunciation
Ц ц	*Ц ц*	ts as in 'tsetse' or tz as in 'blitz'
Ч ч	*Ч ч*	ch as in 'chair'
Ш ш	*Ш ш*	sh as in 'short'
Щ щ	*Щ щ*	shch as in 'fresh-cheese' (run them together)
Ы ы	*ы*	ui as in 'built' (a short 'i', the nearest)
Э э	*Э э*	e as in 'egg'
Ю ю	*Ю ю*	yu as in 'yule'
Я я	*Я я*	ya as in 'yard'

In addition, Russian has two 'mutes' (ь *ь*, ъ *ъ*). These influence the preceding consonant. In the English phonetic spelling the 'soft sign' (ь) will be shown as an apostrophe ('), and if the preceding consonant is pronounced with the merest hint of the 'y' sound as in 'yes' you will get as near as you possibly can to the true sound. The consonant followed by the 'hard sign' (ъ) is simply pronounced with a little more stress. The 'softened' consonants enhance the beauty of the sounds.

Russian vowels are divided into two groups:

Hard: а о у ы э   (a   o   u   ui as in 'built'   e)
Soft: я ё ю и е   (ya   yo   yu   i   ye)

As you see, each hard vowel has a soft vowel as its opposite number.

Now, without preamble, no warning, no advice. The heading of the first chapter is

LET'S GO

You will find separate sections on the more frequently

LET'S GO

used words, mainly verbs and prepositions. Though not intended to be fully comprehensive, these pages should provide an adequate basis for you to be able to speak Russian and encourage you to go on to a more ambitious study of this fascinating language.

Here are few simple sentences. English phonetic pronunciation in brackets.

This is...	Это...	(éto)
a (the) room	комната	(kóm-na-ta)
a (the) hotel	гостиница	(ga-stí-ni-tsa)
a (the) ticket	билет	(bi-lyét)
a (the) key	ключ	(klyúch)
a (the) window	окно	(aknó)
a (the) looking-glass	зеркало	(zyér-ka-lo)

You will have noticed that Russian sentences have no 'a', 'an', 'the' or 'is'. 'Kóm-na-ta' may mean 'a room' or 'the room', depending on the sense.

Now take a good look at the endings of the above words. They are important, as they denote whether a noun is masculine, feminine or neuter. As you see, the first pair end in 'a'. They are *feminine*. The second pair end in a consonant. They are *masculine*. The third pair end in 'o'. They are *neuter*.

This is the basic rule: all nouns ending in a consonant are masculine. Most nouns ending in 'a' are feminine (only a few ending in 'a' are masculine). Almost all nouns ending in 'o' are neuter. All obviously masculine, feminine and neuter nouns present no difficulty but, as there are exceptions to every rule, you will do well to consult a dictionary when

SPEAK, READ, WRITE RUSSIAN

in doubt, as Russian adjectives agree with the nouns they qualify. You will find more information about this in CASES OF NOUNS.

Here are some everyday words to learn right away without waiting for grammatical explanations.

Excuse me, or Sorry	Извините	(Izvinítye)
Please	Пожалуйста	(Pazháluysta)
Give (me, or them, etc.)	Дайте	(Dáytye)
Bring (me, or them, etc.)	Принесите	(Prinyesítye)
Show (me, or them, etc.)	Покажите	(Pakazhítye)
Yes. No.	Да. Нет.	(Da. Nyet.)
Where ...	Где ...	(Gdye)
Now	Сейчас	(Seichás)
Today	Сегодня	(Syevódnya)
Tomorrow	Завтра	(Záftra)
How many or How much	Сколько	(Skól'ko)
Have you ...?	У вас есть ...?	(U vas yést'?)
Here	Здесь	(Zdyes')
There	Там	(Tam)
Thank you	Спасибо	(Spasíbo)

Some Useful Phrases

What is your name?   Как вас зовут?
(*Literally*: How you they call?)   (Kak vas zavút?)

SOME USEFUL PHRASES

What is his name?	Как его зовут? (Kak yevó zavút?)
What is the name of this street?	Как называется эта улица? (Kak nazuiváyetsya éta úlitsa?)
What is this called?	Как называется эта вещь? (Kak nazuiváyetsya éta vyéshch?)
What is that in English?	Как это по-английски? (Kak éto pa-anglíyski?)
How do you spell that? (*Literally*: How that writes itself?)	Как это пишется? (Kak éto píshetsya?)
I am cold. (*Literally*: To me cold.)	Мне холодно. (Mnye khólodno.)
I have a fever.	У меня температура. (U menyá tempyeratúra.)
I have some cigarettes.	У меня есть сигареты. (U menyá yest' sigaryétui.)
I am hungry. (*Literally*: I want to eat.)	Я хочу есть. (Ya khachú yest'.)
I am thirsty.	Я хочу пить. (Ya khachú pit'.)
I am sleepy.	Я хочу спать. (Ya khachú spat'.)
I am in a hurry. (*Literally*: I greatly hasten.)	Я очень тороплюсь. (Ya óchen' taraplyús'.)
We like these rooms.	Нам нравятся эти комнаты. (Nam nrávyatsya éti kómnatui.)

I don't like this restaurant.	Мне не нравится этот ресторан.
	(Mnye nye nrávitsya étot restarán.)
Excuse me, where is the hotel?	Извините, где здесь гостиница?
(*Literally*: Where here hotel?)	(Izvinítye, gdyé zdyés' gastínitsa?)
Have you any (vacant) rooms?	У вас есть свободные комнаты?
	(U vas yést' svabódnuiye kómnatui?)
Show me the room, please.	Покажите, пожалуйста, комнату.
	(Pakazhítye, pazháluysta, kómnatu.)
Give (me) the keys.	Дайте ключи.
(*Literally*: Give keys.)	(Dáytye klyuchí.)
Bring the mirror please.	Принесите, пожалуйста, зеркало.
	(Prinyesítye, pazháluysta, zyérkalo.)

Now a few phrases that you might want to use at a railway station or an airport.

Where is the booking-office?	Где касса?
	(Gdye kássa?)
Show me the time-table.	Покажите мне расписание.
	(Pakazhítye mnyé raspisániye.)
I am going to Leningrad.	Я еду в Ленинград.
	(Ya yédu v Lyeningrát.)

SOME USEFUL PHRASES

Have you tickets?	У вас éсть билéты? (U vas yést' bilyétui?)
You will be going to Leningrad tomorrow.	Вы поéдете в Ленингрáд зáвтра. (Vui payédyetye v Lyeningrát záftra.)
Give (me) one ticket.	Дáйте одúн билéт. (Dáytye adín bilyét.)
Where is the lavatory (toilet)?	Где туалéт? (Gdye tualyét?)
Where is the train?	Где пóезд? (Gdye póyest?)
Where are your tickets?	Где вáши билéты? (Gdye váshi bilyétui?)
Have you finished?	Вы закóнчили? (Vui zakónchili?)
Is everything all right?	Всё в порядке? (Fsyó f paryátkye?)
Please give (me) your passport.	Дáйте, пожáлуйста, ваш пáспорт. (Dáytye, pazháluysta, vash pásport.)
Here it is.	Вóт он. (Vót on.)
Where is the waiting-room/ information office?	Где зал ожидáния/спрáвочное бюрó? (Gdyé zal azhidániya/správochnoye byuró?)
Porter, where is the left-luggage office?	Носúльщик, где кáмера хранéния? (Nasíl'shchik, gdye kámyera khranyéniya?)

SPEAK, READ, WRITE RUSSIAN

In the inquiry-office they will give you all the information you need.
(*Literally*: all necessary information.)

В справочном бюро вам дадут всё нужные справки.
(F správochnom byuró vam dadút vsyé núzhnuiye spráfki.)

Give me a bottle of mineral water, please.

Дайте, пожалуйста, бутылку минеральной воды.
(Dáytye, pazháluysta, butuílku minerál'noy vaduí.)

PLAN OF STUDY

It is a good idea to go right through the book and note where the various grammar sections are located so that you can refer to them as and when you feel you need explanations.

Several pages are devoted to everyday conversation in shops, restaurants, at railway stations, on public transport and at airports. Learn by heart the phrases you feel you will most need and use others as patterns to build sentences of your own with the aid of the relevant grammar sections.

Arrival

Where are the Customs?
Где таможня?
(Gdyé tamózhnya?)

Is this your luggage?
Это ваш багаж?
(Éto vásh bagázh?)

Give me your declaration form.
(*Literally*: Give your declaration.)
Дайте вашу декларацию.
(Dáytye váshu dyeklarátsiyu.)

ARRIVAL

I have some cigarettes.	У меня́ есть сигаре́ты. (U myenyá yest' sigaryétui.)
I have two hundred cigarettes.	У меня́ две́сти сигаре́т. (U myenyá dvyésti sigaryét.)
Is this suitcase yours?	Э́тот чемода́н ва́ш? (Étot chemadán vásh?)
There are only personal possessions here. (*Literally*: Here only personal possessions.)	Здесь то́лько ли́чные ве́щи. (Zdyes' tól'ko líchnuiye vyéshchi.)
Please open it.	Откро́йте, пожа́луйста. (Atkróytye, pazháluysta.)
Here are the keys.	Во́т ключи́. (Vót klyuchí.)
Let me see what that is.	Разреши́те посмотре́ть, что́ э́то тако́е. (Razreshítye pasmotryét', shtó éto takóye.)
How much must I pay?	Ско́лько я до́лжен заплати́ть? (Skól'ka ya dólzhen zaplatít'?)
There is nothing to pay on this.	За э́то не ну́жно ничего́ плати́ть. (Za éto nye núzhno nichevó platít'.)
Excuse me, shall we be kept here long?	Извини́те, до́лго ли нас здесь заде́ржат? (Izvinítye, dólgo li nas zdyés' zadyérzhat?)

The Hotel

Have you any accommodation?	У вас есть свободные комнаты?
(*Literally*: With you are free rooms?)	(U vas yést' svabódnuiye kómnatui?)
What kind of room would you like?	Какую комнату вы хотели бы?
	(Kakúyu kómnatu vui khatyéli bui?)
I want a room on the first floor.	Я хочу комнату на втором этаже.
(*Literally*: ... on the second floor.)	(Ya khachú kómnatu na ftaróm etazhé.)

Note that the Russian way of counting the floors differs from the English. The first floor corresponds to the English ground floor, and so in Russian, as on the Continent generally, each floor is one number higher than in English.

There are two of us.	Нас двое.
(*Literally*: We are two.)	(Nas dvóye.)
We shall stay a week.	Мы пробудем неделю.
	(Mui prabúdyem nyedélyu.)
And what is the price?	А какая цена?
	(A kakáya tsyená?)
Four roubles a night.	Четыре рубля в сутки.
	(Chetuírye rublyá v sútki.)

The Russian word 'sútki' has no precise English translation; it means a 24-hour day-and-night period.

That is not expensive.	Это недорого.
	(Éto nyedórago.)

THE HOTEL

That will suit us.	Это нам подойдёт.
	(Éto nam padaydyót.)
I think that the room will please you.	Я думаю, что комната вам понравится.
	(Ya dúmayu, shto kómnata vam panrávitsya.)
Show us the room please.	Покажите нам комнату, пожалуйста.
	(Pokazhítye nam kómnatu, pazháluysta.)

'Kómnata' (room) is the subject of the first of the two preceding sentences. The ending '-a' shows that it is in the *Nominative Case*. But in the second sentence it is the object, i.e. the thing being shown. The ending '-y' indicates that it is in the *Accusative Case*. The cases are an important feature of Russian nouns. For further details see CASES OF NOUNS.

No, I do not like the room. (*Literally*: No, this room does not please me.)	Нет, эта комната мне не нравится.
	(Nyet, éta kómnata mnye nye nrávitsya.)
May (we) see another room?	Можно посмотреть другую комнату?
	(Mózhno pasmatryét' druguyu kómnatu?)
We will take this room.	Мы возьмём эту комнату.
	(Mui vazmyóm étu kómnatu.)
Please wait a little.	Пожалуйста, подождите немного.
	(Pazháluysta, padazhdítye nyemnógo.)

SPEAK, READ, WRITE RUSSIAN

Fill in this form.	Заполните этот бланк.
	(Zapólnitye étot blank.)
Sign here.	Распишитесь здесь.
	(Raspishítyes' zdyés'.)
All the formalities are completed.	Все формальности закончены.
	(Fsyé formál'nosti zakónchenui.)
Here is your key; room number twenty-two, first floor.	Вот ваш ключ: комната номер двадцать-два, второй этаж.
	(Vót vash klyúch: kómnata nómyer dvát-tsat'-dva, ftarói etázh.)
Where are you living now?	Где вы сейчас живёте?
	(Gdye vui seichás zhivyótye?)
We are staying at the 'Minsk' Hotel.	Мы живём в гостинице «Минск».
(*Literally*: We are living...)	(Mui zhivyóm v gastínitse 'Minsk'.)
Wake us at eight, please.	Разбудите нас в восемь часов, пожалуйста.
	(Razbudítye nas v vósyem' chasóv, pazháluysta.)
We are leaving this evening.	Мы уезжаем сегодня вечером.
	(Mui uyezháyem syevódnya vyécherom.)
Bring (me) the bill, please.	Принесите мне счёт, пожалуйста.
	(Prinyesítye mnye shchót, pazháluysta.)

A SIMPLE VERB

There are two or more Russian verbs of the same root (or stem) which correspond to each English verb. Broadly speaking, every Russian verb has two infinitives, depending on the nature of the action. In grammatical terms they are called ASPECTS and are the IMPERFECTIVE ASPECT (present, past and future) and the PERFECTIVE ASPECT (past and future—no present). It is a great help if *both aspects are learned simultaneously*.

The IMPERFECTIVE denotes that the ACTION is of an *indefinite, continued nature*—it is repeated or may be repeated.

The PERFECTIVE, as the word implies, denotes that the action was of a *definite* or *complete* nature, or that it will be *completed* soon. This PERFECTIVE is formed from the IMPERFECTIVE either by prefixing a preposition, or by changing a vowel or syllable.

As you progress you will be delighted to discover that you can enrich your vocabulary simply by adding various prefixes to verbs. Don't worry at this stage, however, as you will find more details later on.

Note that 'ты' (tui)—'thou', the second person singular is only used when speaking to children, relatives and close friends.

Let us take the verb 'to begin'. In English it stands for beginning once or beginning time and again. In Russian you will know exactly whether it is a repeated action or not.

To Begin—**Начинáть** (Nachinát')

Imperfective
I begin я начинáю (ya nachináyu)

he, she, it begins	он, она́, оно́ начина́ет	(on, oná, anó nachináyet)
we begin	мы начина́ем	(mui nachináyem)
you begin	вы начина́ете	(vui nachináyetye)
they begin	они́ начина́ют	(aní nachináyut)

Perfective: **Нача́ть** (Nachát')

I shall begin	я начну́	(ya nachnú)
he, she, it will begin	он, она́, оно́ начнёт	(on, oná, onó nachnyót)
we shall begin	мы начнём	(mui nachnyóm)
you will begin	вы начнёте	(vui nachnyótye)
they will begin	они́ начну́т	(aní nachnút)

Throughout this book IMPERFECTIVE verbs will be marked 'Imperf.' and PERFECTIVE verbs 'Perf.'

AT (idiomatic use)

When referring to space: в (v, f), на (na), у (u).
When referring to time: в (v, f).

The train arrives *at* the Alexandrov station.
По́езд прибыва́ет *на* ста́нцию Алекса́ндров.
(Póyezd pribuiváyet *na* stántsiyu Aleksándrof.)

They are staying *at* the 'National' Hotel.
Они́ живу́т *в* гости́нице «Национа́ль».
(Aní zhivút *v* gástinitse 'Natsionál'.)

We shall return *at* three o'clock.
Мы вернёмся *в* три часа́.
(Mui vyernyómsya *v* tri chasá.)

Yesterday we were *at* my friend's (house).
Вчера́ мы бы́ли у моего́ дру́га.
(Fcherá mui buíli *u* mayevó drúga.)

But note, the phrase: Will you be *at* home?—Вы бу́дете до́ма? (Vui búdetye dóma?) does not use the preposition.

To Be—Быть (buit')

Present: есть (yest')
Past: был (buil) (m.), была́ (builá) (f.),
  бы́ло (builó) (n.), бы́ли (buíli) (pl.)
Future: я бу́ду   (ya búdu)
  он, она́ бу́дет   (on, oná búdyet)
  мы бу́дем   (mui búdyem)
  вы бу́дете   (vui búdyetye)
  они́ бу́дут   (aní búdut)

The verb 'есть' (yest') is usually omitted in the Present Tense.

I am a tourist.	Я тури́ст. (Ya turíst.)
We are from England.	Мы из А́нглии. (Mui iz Ánglii.)
Here is my passport.	Во́т мой па́спорт. (Vót moi pásport.)

In the Past Tense the verb agrees with the subject in both gender and number.

My father was a driver.
Мой оте́ц был шофёром.
(Moi atyéts buil shafyórom.)

My wife has not been to Leningrad.
Моя́ жена́ не́ была́ в Ленингра́де.
(Mayá zhená nyé builá v Leningrádye.)

We have already been to the Bolshoi Theatre.	Мы ужé бы́ли в Большóм теáтре.
	(Mui uzhé buíli v Bal'shóm te-átrye.)

The verb 'быть' (to be) used in the Future Tense both independently and as an auxiliary helps form the future tense of imperfective verbs.

You will be in London in three hours.	Вы бу́дете в Лóндоне чéрез три часá.
(*Literally*: ... after three hours.)	(Vui búdyetye v Lóndonye chéryez tri chasá.)
You will speak Russian well in three months (time).	Вы бу́дете хорошó говори́ть по-ру́сски чéрез три мéсяца.
	(Vui búdyetye kharashó gavarít' pa-rússki chéryez tri mésyatsa.)

To see how the verb 'есть' is used to denote possession, study TO HAVE and POSSESSION.

Before

In time: рáньше (rán'she), прéжде (pryézhdye).

Before—прéжде чем (pryézhdye chem), дó (dó).

I should like to meet you before you leave.	Я хотéл бы встрéтиться с вáми до отъéзда.
(*Literally*: ... before departure.)	(Ya khatyél bui fstryétitsya s vámi da atyézda.)
Phone me before you come out.	Прéжде чем éхать, позвони́те мне по телефóну.
	(Pryézhdye chem yékhat', pozvoníte mnye pa tyelyefónu.)

BEFORE

What was this building before?	Что было в этом здании раньше?
(*Literally*: What was in . . .?)	(Shto búilo v étom zdánii rán'she?)
This building used to be a church, now it is a museum.	Раньше в этом здании была церковь, а теперь здесь музей.
(*Literally*: There was a church in this building before, and now a museum is here.)	(Rán'she v étom zdánii buíla tsérkof', a tyepyér' zdyes' muzyéi.)

Bring

Imperf. **Приносить** (prinasít')
Present:

I bring	я приношу	(ya prinashú)
you bring	вы приносите	(vui prinósitye)
they bring	они приносят	(aní prinósyat)

Future:

| I shall bring | я буду приносить | (ya búdu prinasít') |

Past (repeated or incompleted action):

I brought	я приносил	(ya prinasíl) (m.)
I brought	я приносила	(ya prinasíla (f.)
we brought	мы приносили	(mui prinasíli) (pl.)

Perf. **Принести** (prinyestí)
Future:

I will bring	я принесу	(ya prinyesú)
you will bring	вы принесёте	(vui prinyesyótye)
they will bring	они принесут	(aní prinyesút)

Past (action that took place only once; completed action):

| I brought | я принёс | (ya prinyós) (m.) |

SPEAK, READ, WRITE RUSSIAN

| I brought | я принесла́ | (ya prinyeslá) (f.) |
| we brought | мы принесли́ | (mui prinyeslí) (pl.) |

Imperative: Принеси́те (Prinyesítye)

Newspapers are brought early in the morning.	Газе́ты прино́сят ра́но у́тром. (Gazyétui prinósyat ráno útrom.)
Bring the tickets, please.	Принеси́те, пожа́луйста, биле́ты. (Prinyesítye, pazháluysta, bilyétui.)
We shall bring them tomorrow.	Мы принесём их за́втра. (Mui prinyesyóm ikh záftra.)
I have brought you an interesting book.	Я принёс вам интере́сную кни́гу. (Ya prinyós vam intyeryésnuyu knígu.)

Can—May—Be Able

Imper. **Мочь** (moch').
Present:

I can (may)	я могу́	(ya magú)
you can (may)	вы мо́жете	(vui mózhetye)
they can (may)	они́ мо́гут	(aní mógut)

Past:

I could	я мог	(mog) (m.)
	я могла́	(maglá) (f.)
Plurals:	могли́	(maglí)

26

CAN—MAY—BE ABLE

Perf. Смочь (smoch')
Future:

I will be able	я смогу́	(ya smagú)
you will be able	вы смо́жете	(vui smózhetye)
they will be able	они́ смо́гут	(ani smógut)

Can you recommend a good restaurant?
(*Literally*: Can you recommend to us . . .?)

Вы мо́жете порекомендова́ть нам хоро́ший рестора́н?
(Vui mózhetye parekomyendovát' nam kharóshiy restarán?)

I cannot answer your question.

Я не могу́ отве́тить на ваш вопро́с.
(Ya nye magú atvyétit' na vásh vaprós.)

Forgive me, I could not come yesterday.

Извини́те, вчера́ я не мог прие́хать.
(Izvinítye, fcherá ya nye mog priyékhat'.)

Ring me from Kiev if you can.

Е́сли смо́жете, позвони́те мне из Ки́ева.
(Yésli smózhetye, pazvanítye mnye iz Kíyeva.)

To Ask Permission
'Мо́жно' (mózhno)—'may one':

May I(we) come in?
Мо́жно войти́?
(Mózhno vaytí?)

Can we ring London from here?
Здесь мо́жно позвони́ть в Ло́ндон?
(Zdyes' mózhno pazvanít v Lóndon?)

When something is forbidden they say:

'нельзя' (nyel'zyá)—'one must not'

You must (may) not smoke.	Вам нельзя курить.
	(Vam nyel'zyá kurít').
You must not park here. (*Literally*: You must not place (your) car here.)	Здесь нельзя ставить машину.
	(Zdyes' nyel'zyá stávit' mashínu.)

'Mashína', the literal translation of which is machine, is the accepted colloquial word for motorcar in Russia.

CONJUNCTIONS

Most Russian conjunctions are used in the same way as their English counterparts. The only difficulty may be with '*a*', which may correspond to either 'and' or 'but'. It depends on the sense of the phrase.

и (i)—and
а (a)—and, but
но (no)—but
или (íli)—or
если (yésli)—if
чем (chem)—than
потому что (patamú shto)—because

I speak English and German and my wife speaks English and French.	Я говорю по-английски и по-немецки, а моя жена говорит по-английски и по-французски.
	(Ya gavaryú pa-anglíyski i pa-nyemyétski, a mayá zhená gavarít pa-anglíyski i pa-frantsúski.)
I understand Russian, but my wife does not.	Я понимаю по-русски, а моя жена нет.
	(Ya panimáyu pa-rússki, a mayá zhená nyet.)

CONJUNCTIONS

Examples with other conjunctions:

Tomorrow we'll go to Suzdal or to Zagorsk.	Завтра мы поедем в Суздаль или в Загорск.
	(Záftra mui payédyem f Súzdal' íli v Zagórsk.)
We have bought (some) books and records.	Мы купили книги и пластинки.
	(Mui kupíli knígi i plastínki.)
I would very much like to go to the Exhibition, but today I am busy.	Я очень хочу поехать на выставку, но сегодня я занят.
	(Ya óchen' khachú payékhat' na vuístafku, no syevódnya ya zányat.)
He cannot go to the Exhibition because he is busy.	Он не может поехать на выставку, потому что он занят.
	(On nye mózhet payékhat' na vuístafku, patamú shto on zányat.)

To Eat

Imperf. Есть (yest')
Present:
  я ем, ты ешь, он ест, мы едим, вы едите, они едят
  (ya yem, tui yesh', on yest, mui yedím, vui yedítye, aní yedyát)
  (I eat, thou eatest, etc.) See note regarding the use of the second person singular, on p. 23.

Perf. Поесть (payést')
Past:
  ел (yel) (m.)   ела (yéla) (f.)   ели (yéli) (pl.)

Future: I will eat	я бу́ду есть (ya búdu yest')
you will eat	вы бу́дете есть (vui búdyetye yest')
we will eat	мы бу́дем есть (mui búdyem yest')
I am hungry.	Я хочу́ есть.
(*Literally*: I want to eat.)	(Ya khachú yest'.)
Will you eat now?	Вы бу́дете сейча́с есть?
	(Vui búdyetye seichás yest'?)
We shall not eat; we have already eaten.	Мы не бу́дем есть; мы уже́ е́ли.
	(Mui nye búdyem yest'; mui uzhé yéli.)

Imperf. за́втракать (záftrakat')—to have breakfast.
Perf. поза́втракать (pazáftrakat')—to have breakfast.
Imperf. обе́дать (abyédat')—to have dinner.
Perf. пообе́дать (pa-abyédat')—to have dinner.
Imperf. у́жинать (úzhinat')—to have supper.
Perf. поу́жинать (pa-úzhinat')—to have supper.

Eating

We are hungry.	Мы хоти́м есть.
	(Mui khatím yest'.)
Can you recommend a good restaurant?	Вы мо́жете порекомендова́ть хоро́ший рестора́н?
	(Vui mózhetye parekomendovát' kharóshiy restarán?)
There is a very good restaurant nearby. It is the 'Ukraina' restaurant.	Здесь недалеко́ о́чень хоро́ший рестора́н. Э́то рестора́н «Украи́на».
	(Zdyes' nyedalyekó óchen' kharóshiy restarán. Éto restarán 'Ukraína'.

30

EATING

That's fine. (Very good.) We shall go there now.	Очень хорошо. Мы сейчас туда пойдём. (Óchen' kharashó. Mui seichás tudá paydyóm.)
Good afternoon. We should like a table for four.	Добрый день. Мы хотели бы столик для четверых. (Dóbruiy den'. Mui khatyéli bui stólik dlya chetvyeruíkh.)
Is this table free?	Этот стол свободен? (Étot stol svabódyen?)
This table is occupied, but that one is free.	Этот стол занят, а тот свободен. (Étot stol zányat, a tot svabódyen.)
Where can we wash our hands? (*Literally*: Where may hands be washed?)	Где можно помыть руки? (Gdye mózhno pamuít' rúki?)
We wish to have breakfast (dinner, supper).	Мы хотим позавтракать (пообедать, поужинать). (Mui khatím pazáftrakat' (pa-abyédat', pa-úzhinat'.)
The menu, please.	Меню, пожалуйста. (Menyú, pazháluysta.)
Let me have a meat dish, please. (*Literally*: Give me, please, ...)	Дайте, пожалуйста, мясное блюдо. (Dáytye, pazháluysta, myasnóye blyúdo.)

I would recommend (to) you a shashlik.	Я бы вам рекомендовал шашлык.
	(Ya bui vam rekomendavál shashluík.)
And I prefer fish.	А я предпочитаю рыбу.
	(A yá pretpachitáyu ruíbu.)
We have very good icecream.	У нас очень хорошее мороженое.
(*Literally*: Our icecream is very good.)	(U nas óchen' kharósheye morózhenoye.)
What shall we drink?	Что мы будем пить?
	(Shto mui búdyem pit'?)
Two hundred grammes of vodka and a bottle of dry wine for us, please.	Нам, пожалуйста, двести грамм водки и бутылку сухого вина.
	(Nam, pazháluysta, dvyésti gram vótki i butuílku sukhóvo viná.)
(And) the same for us.	Нам то же самое.
	(Nam to zhe sámoye.)
Bon appetit!	Приятного аппетита!
	(Priyátnavo appyetíta!)
Your health!	За ваше здоровье!
	(Za váshe zdaróv'ye!)
The bill, please.	Счёт, пожалуйста.
	(Shchót, pazháluysta.)
Do come again.	Приходите к нам ещё раз.
(*Literally*: Come to us again.)	(Prikhadítye k nam yeshchó raz.)

EATING

Thank you, we will. (*Literally*: Thank you, we shall come without fail.)	Спасибо, обязательно придём. (Spasíbo, obyazátel'no pridyóm.)

Enquiries

Tell me, please, where is Revolution Square?	Скажите, пожалуйста, где Площадь Революции? (Skazhítye, pazháluysta, gdyé plóshchat' Ryevolyútsii?)
Go straight ahead and (then) left.	Идите прямо и налево. (Idítye pryámo i nalyévo.)
Sorry, I don't know. Ask someone else. (*Literally*: ... Ask another.)	Простите, я не знаю. Спросите другого. (Prastítye, ya nye znáyu. Sprasítye drugóvo.)
Which trolleybus goes to the 'Rossia' Hotel?	Какой троллейбус идёт до гостиницы «Россия»? (Kakói trallèybus idyót do gastínitsui 'Rassiya'?)
Does bus Number 5 go there?	Автобус номер пять идёт туда? (Aftóbus nómyer pyat' idyót tudá?)
Where is the No. 25 trolleybus stop?	Где остановка троллейбуса номер двадцать пять? (Gdyé astanófka trallèybusa nómyer dváttsat' pyát'?)
What is the name of this street?	Как называется эта улица? (Kak nazuiváyetsya éta úlitsa?)

Where is the Service Bureau?	Где бюро́ обслу́живания? (Gdye byuró apslúzhivaniya?)
What is this called?	Как э́то называ́ется? (Kak éto nazuiváyetsya?)
What is this in English?	Как э́то по-англи́йски? (Kak éto pa-anglíyski?)
What does this word mean in Russian?	Что зна́чит э́то сло́во по-ру́сски? (Shto znáchit éto slóvo parússki?)
Show (me) this word in the dictionary.	Покажи́те э́то сло́во в слова́ре́. (Pokazhítye éto slóvo f slovaryé.)
What is the Russian for . . . ? (*Literally*: How in Russian?)	Как по-ру́сски . . . ? (Kak pa-rússki . . . ?)
Have you an English-Russian dictionary?	У вас есть а́нгло-ру́сский слова́рь? (U vas yést' ángla-rússkiy slovár'?)
I have a Russian-English dictionary.	У меня́ есть ру́сско-англи́йский слова́рь. (U myenyá yest' rússka-anglíyskiy slovár'.)
Do you understand me?	Вы понима́ете меня́? (Vui panimáyetye myenyá?)
I don't understand you entirely.	Я не совсе́м вас понима́ю. (Ya nye safsyém vas panimáyu.)

ENQUIRIES

Do you speak English?	Вы говори́те по-англи́йски?
	(Vui gavarítye pa-anglíyski?)
I have lost my way.	Я заблуди́лся. (m.) or
	Я заблуди́лась. (f.)
	(Ya zabludílsya (m.) or
	Ya zabludílas' (f.).)
We have lost our way.	Мы заблуди́лись. (pl.)
	(Mui zabludílis'.)
We are looking for the Hotel 'National'.	Мы и́щем гости́ницу «Национа́ль».
	(Mui íshchyem gastínitsu 'Natsionál'.)
Where is the nearest post office?	Где ближа́йшая по́чта?
	(Gdye blizháyshaya póchta?)

The simplest way to ask a question is with intonation. Note carefully how this can be done:

Statement: This is a hotel. Э́то гости́ница.
(Éto gastínitsa.)

Question: Is this a hotel? Э́то гости́ница?
(Éto gastínitsa?)

Statement: That is your luggage. Э́то ваш бага́ж.
(Éto vásh bagázh.)

Question: Is that your luggage? Э́то ваш бага́ж?
(Éto vásh bagázh?)

Statement:
You have been to the (sports) stadium. Вы бы́ли на стадио́не.
(Vui buíli na stadiónye.)

Question:
Have you been to the (sports) stadium? Вы бы́ли на стадио́не?
(Vui buíli na stadiónye?)

Russians rarely preface the word 'sports' to stadium. The word is implied but not stated.

A question can also be constructed with the help of the particle 'ли' (li) placed after the main word in the question. This is used mainly for emphasis.

Have you been to the stadium?	Бы́ли ли вы на стадио́не? (Buíli li vui na stadiónye?)
Is this a hotel?	Гости́ница ли э́то? (Gastínitsa li éto?)
Shall we be kept here long?	До́лго ли нас здесь заде́ржат? (Dòlgo li nas zdyes' zadyérzhat'?)

Many questions begin with an interrogative word (see under INTERROGATIVES).

Who can help us?	Кто мо́жет нам помо́чь? (Kto mózhet nam pamóch'?)
What do you want to do?	Что вы хоти́те сде́лать? (Shto vui khatítye zdyélat'?)
Where did you buy the 'Leningrad Ballet' album?	Где вы купи́ли альбо́м «Ленингра́дский бале́т?» (Gdye vui kupili al'bóm 'Lyeningrátskiy balyét'?)

Replies can be long or short. The shortest answer to a general question is 'Да' (Da), yes, or 'Нет' (Nyet), no.

Do you speak English? Yes.	Вы говори́те по-англи́йски? Да. (Vui gavarítye pa-anglíyski? Da.)

ENQUIRIES

Do you want to go to the theatre? No.	Вы хотите пойти в театр? Нет.
	(Vui khatítye paytí f te-átr? Nyet.)
Have you bought (any) records? Yes.	Вы купили пластинки? Да.
	(Vui kupíli plastínki? Da.)
Did you buy the records yesterday? No.	Вы купили пластинки вчера? Нет.
	(Vui kupíli plastínki fcherá? Nyet.)

Here is another example of the short reply:

Do you speak English?	Вы говорите по-английски?
	(Vui gavarítye pa-anglíyski?)
Yes, I do. (short)	Да, говорю.
(*Literally*: Yes, I speak.)	(Da, gavaryú.)
or	
Yes, I speak English. (long)	Да, я говорю по-английски.
	(Da, ya gavaryú pa-anglíyski.)
Do you want to go to the theatre?	Вы хотите пойти в театр?
	(Vui khatítye paytí f te-átr?)
No, I don't. (short)	Нет, не хочу.
(*Literally*: No, I don't want to.	(Nyet, nye khachú.)
or	
No, I don't want to go to the theatre. (long)	Нет, я не хочу итти в театр.
	(Nyet, ya nye khachú ittí f te-átr.)

Have you bought records?	Вы купи́ли пласти́нки?
	(Vui kupíli plastínki?)
Yes, I have. (short)	Да, пласти́нки.
(*Literally*: Yes, records.)	(Da, plastínki.)
or	
Yes, I've bought (some) records. (long)	Да, я купи́л пласти́нки. (m.)
	(Da, ya kupíl plastínki.)
Did you buy the records yesterday?	Вы купи́ли пласти́нки вчера́?
	(Vui kupíli plastínki fcherá?)
No, not yesterday. (short)	Нет, не вчера́.
	(Nyet, nye fcherá.)
or	
No, I did not buy the records yesterday. I bought them the day before yesterday. (long)	Нет, я купи́л пласти́нки не вчера́, я купи́л их позавчера́. (m.)
	(Nyet, ya kupíl plastínki nye fcherá, ya kupíl ikh pozafcherá.)

A short specific answer to a specific question.

What have you bought?	Что́ вы купи́ли?
	(Shtó vui kupíli?)
A picture book, 'The Moscow Kremlin'.	Альбо́м «Моско́вский Кре́мль».
	(Al'bóm 'Maskófskiy Kryéml' '.)
Where are you going tomorrow?	Куда́ вы пое́дете за́втра?
	(Kudá vui payédyetye záftra?)
To Leningrad.	В Ленигра́д.
	(V Lyeningrát.)

ENQUIRIES

Where will you be on Sunday?	Где вы бу́дете в воскресе́нье?
	(Gdye vui búdyetye v vaskryesyénye?)
In Leningrad.	В Ленингра́де.
	(V Lyeningrádye.)

To Read

Imperf. **Чита́ть** (chitát')

Present: I read   я чита́ю   (ya chitáyu)
          you read   вы чита́ете   (vui chitáyetye)
          they read   они́ чита́ют   (aní chitáyut)

Future: I shall read   я бу́ду чита́ть
                       (ya búdu chitát')
        you will read   вы бу́дете чита́ть
                       (vui búdyete chitát')
        he will read   он бу́дет чита́ть
                       (on búdyet chitát')
        we shall read   мы бу́дем чита́ть
                       (mui búdyem chitát')
        they will read   они́ бу́дут чита́ть
                       (aní búdut chitát')

Past: I/he read   я/он чита́л   (m.)
                       (ya/on chitál)
        I/she read   я/она́ чита́ла   (f.)
                       (ya/oná chitála)
        we/they read   мы/они́ чита́ли   (pl.)
                       (mui/aní chitáli)

Imperative: Read (please)!   Чита́йте!   (Chitáytye!)

We read English and American newspapers.	Мы читáем англи́йские и америкáнские газéты.
	(Mui chitáyem anglíyskiye i amyerikánskiye gazyétui.)
I shall soon be able to read Russian.	Скóро я бýду читáть по-рýсски.
(*Literally*: Soon I shall read in Russian.)	(Skóro ya búdu chitát' parússki.)
Have you read this book?	Вы читáли э́ту кни́гу?
	(Vui chitáli etu knígu?)
I have not yet read these magazines.	Я ещё не читáла э́ти журнáлы. (f.)
	(Ya yeshchó nye chitála éti zhurnálui.)

To Reply, To Answer

Imperf. **Отвечáть** (atvyechát')

Present:

I reply	я отвечáю	(ya atvyecháyu)
you reply	вы отвечáете	(vui atvyecháyetye)
he replies	он отвечáет	(on atvyecháyet)
we reply	мы отвечáем	(mui atvyecháyem)
they reply	они́ отвечáют	(aní atvyecháyut)

Perf. **Отвéтить** (atvyétit')

Future:

I will reply	я отвéчу	(ya atvyéchu)
you will reply	вы отвéтите	(vui atvyétitye)
he will reply	он отвéтит	(on atvyétit)
we will reply	мы отвéтим	(mui atvyétim)
they will reply	они́ отвéтят	(aní atvyétyat)

TO REPLY, TO ANSWER

Past:
I/he replied	я/он отве́тил (m.)
	(ya/on atvyétil)
I/she replied	я/она́ отве́тила (f.)
	(ya/oná atvyétila)
we/they replied	мы они́ отве́тили (pl.)
	(mui/aní atvyétili)

Why do you not answer?	Почему́ вы не отвеча́ете?
	(Pachyemú vui nye atvyecháyete?)
I can't answer your question.	Я не могу́ отве́тить на ваш вопро́с.
	(Ya nye magú atvyétit' na vash vaprós.)
What did he answer you?	Что он вам отве́тил?
	(Shto on vam atvyétil?)
We will reply to this telegram tomorrow.	Мы отве́тим на э́ту телегра́мму за́втра.
	(Mui atvyétim na étu tyelyegrámu záftra.)

To Say, To Tell, To Speak

Imperf. Говори́ть (gavarít')

Present:
I speak	я говорю́	(ya gavaryú)
you speak	вы говори́те	(vui gavarítye)
he speaks	он говори́т	(on gavarít)
we speak	мы говори́м	(mui gavarím)
they speak	они́ говоря́т	(aní gavaryát)

Past:
| I/he said | я/он говори́л | (ya/on gavaríl) (m.) |

SPEAK, READ, WRITE RUSSIAN

I/she said	я/она́ говори́ла (f.)
	(ya oná gavaríla)
we/they said	мы/они́ говори́ли (pl.)
	(mui/aní gavaríli)

Perf. Сказа́ть (skazát')
Future:

I shall say	я скажу́	(ya skazhú)
you will say	вы ска́жете	(vui skázhetye)
he will say	он ска́жет	(on skázhet)
we shall say	мы ска́жем	(mui skázhem)
they will say	они́ ска́жут	(aní skázhut)

Past:

I/he said	я/он сказа́л (m.)
	(ya/on skazál)
I/she said	я/она́ сказа́ла (f.)
	(ya/oná skazála)
we/you said	мы/вы сказа́ли (pl.)
	(mui/vui skazáli)

Imperative: Speak! **Скажи́те!** (Skazhítye!)

What is he saying?	Что он говори́т?
	(Shto on gavarít?)
What have you been talking (about?)	О чём вы говори́ли?
	(A chóm vui gavaríli?)
Excuse me, what did you say?	Прости́те, что́ вы сказа́ли?
	(Prastítye, shtó vui skazáli?)
Tell me, what is that?	Скажи́те, что́ э́то тако́е?
	(Skazhítye, shtó éto takóye?)
I'll tell you about it tomorrow.	Я вам скажу́ об э́том за́втра.
	(Ya vam skazhú ab étom záftra.)

To See

Imperf. Ви́деть (vídyet')

Present:
I see	я ви́жу	(ya vízhu)
you see	вы ви́дите	(vui víditye)
he sees	он ви́дит	(on vídit)
we see	мы ви́дим	(mui vídim)
they see	они́ ви́дят	(aní vídyat)

Past:
I/he saw	я/он ви́дел (m.)	(ya/on vídyel)
I/she saw	я/она́ ви́дела (f.)	(ya/oná vídyela)
we/you saw	мы/вы ви́дели. (pl)	(mui/vui vídyeli)

Perf. Уви́деть (uvídyet')

Future:
I will see	я уви́жу	(ya uvízhu)
you will see	вы уви́дете	(vui uvídyetye)
he will see	он уви́дит	(on uvídit)
we will see	мы уви́дим	(mui uvídim)
they will see	они́ уви́дят	(aní uvídyat)

I don't see very well (I have weak eyesight.) (*Literally*: I see badly.)	Я пло́хо ви́жу. (Ya plókho vízhu.)
Do you see that large house (over there)?	Вы ви́дите тот большо́й дом? (Vui víditye tot bal'shói dom?)
We have seen this/that film.	Мы ви́дели э́тот фильм. (Mui vídyeli étot fil'm.)

SPEAK, READ, WRITE RUSSIAN

When will you see your friend?	Когда́ вы уви́дите своего́ дру́га?
	(Kagdá vui uvíditye svayevó drúga?)
I will see him tomorrow.	Я уви́жу его́ за́втра.
	(Ya uvízhu yevó záftra.)
I am glad to see you.	Я рад вас ви́деть. (m.)
	(Ya rat vas vídyet'.)

Shopping

Let's go to the shop.	Дава́йте пойдём в магази́н.
	(Daváytye paydyóm v magazín.)
I want to buy some souvenirs.	Я хочу́ купи́ть сувени́ры.
	(Ya khachú kupít' suvyenírui.)
Where is the nearest souvenir shop?	Где ближа́йший магази́н сувени́ров?
	(Gdye blizháyshiy magazín suvyenírof?)
'Souvenirs' shop is on Gorky Street.	Магази́н «Сувени́ры» нахо́дится на у́лице Го́рького.
	(Magazín 'Suvyenírui' nakhóditsya ya úlitsye Górkavo.)
There are good souvenirs in the 'Beriozka' shop.	Хоро́шие сувени́ры есть в магази́не «Берёзка».
	(Kharóshiye suvyenírui yest' v magazínye 'Byeryóska.')
Can you use English money there?	Там мо́жно плати́ть англи́йскими деньга́ми?
(*Literally*: May one pay there with English money?)	(Tam mózhno platít' anglíyskimi dyen'gámi?)

SHOPPING

What are its hours of opening?
(*Literally*: During what hours does it work?)

В какие часы работает этот магазин?
(F kakíye chasuí rabótayet étot magazín?)

This shop is open from 11.00 hours to 20.00 hours.

Этот магазин работает с одиннадцати до двадцати.
(Étot magazín rabótayet s adínnattsati do dvattsatí.)

What would you like to buy?

Что вы хотите купить?
(Shto vui khatítye kupít'?)

We should like to buy Russian souvenirs.

Мы хотели бы купить русские сувениры.
(Mui khatyéli bui kupít' rússkiye suvyenírui.)

We have silver, amber, lace, caskets, dolls.
(*Literally*: Please, here is silver, etc.)

Пожалуйста, вот серебро, янтарь, кружево, шкатулки, куклы.
(Pazháluysta, vot syeryebró, yantár', krúzhevo, shkatúlki, kúklui.)

Do you have badges?

У вас есть значки?
(U vas yést' znachkí?)

I should like to buy long-playing records. (f.)

Я хотела бы купить долгоиграющие пластинки.
(Ya khatyéla bui kupít' dolgoigráyushchiye plastínki.)

How much does this cost?

Сколько это стоит?
(Skól'ko eto stó-it?)

Our books and records are very good and inexpensive.

Пластинки и книги у нас очень хорошие и недорогие.
(Plastínki i knígi u nas óchen' kharóshiye i nyedaragíye.)

I like this.	Мне нра́вится э́то.
	(Mnye nrávitsya éto.)
Do you like that?	Вам э́то нра́вится?
	(Vam éto nrávitsya?)
That is very expensive.	Э́то о́чень до́рого.
	(Éto óchen' dórogo.)
Show me a fur hat.	Покажи́те мне мехову́ю ша́пку.
	(Pokazhítye mnye myekhavúyu shápku.)
Which one? This one?	Каку́ю? Э́ту?
	(Kakúyu? Étu?)
No, that one, please.	Нет, ту́, пожа́луйста.
	(Nyet, tú, pazháluysta.)
I should like to try it on.	Я хоте́ла бы пример́ить её. (f.)
	(Ya khatyéla bui primyerít' yeyó.)
How much is this hat? (*Literally*: How much to pay for this hat?)	Ско́лько плати́ть за э́ту ша́пку?
	(Skól'ko platít' za étu shápku?)
Eleven roubles sixty copeks.	Оди́ннадцать рубле́й шестьдеся́т копе́ек.
	(Adínnattsat' rublyéi shest'dyesyát kapéyek.)
It is not dear.	Э́то недо́рого.
	(Éto nyedórogo.)
I should like to buy a large nest of dolls.	Я хоте́л бы купи́ть большу́ю матрёшку. (m.)
	(Ya khatyél bui kupít' bal'shúyu matryóshku.)

SHOPPING

I am sorry, but we have sold out of large nests of dolls. (*Literally*: Regrettably, large nests of dolls have been sold out today.)	К сожалéнию, большие матрёшки сегóдня прóданы. (K sozhalyéniyu, bal'shíye matryóshki syevódnya pródanui.)

'Matryóshka' is the name given to the popular folk toy, a nest of dolls.

Come tomorrow.	Приходи́те зáвтра. (Prikhadítye záftra.)
Pay at the cash desk.	Плати́те в кáссу. (Platítye f kássu.)
Here is your change. (*Literally*: Receive change.)	Получи́те сдáчу. (Paluchítye sdáchu.)

Sightseeing

Where is the service bureau?	Где бюрó обслýживания? (Gdye byuró apslúzhivaniya?)
We should like to go on a tour to ... (*Literally*: ... excursion)	Мы хотéли бы пойти́ (поéхать) на экскýрсию в ... (Mui khatyéli bui paytí (payékhat') na ekskúrsiyu v ...)
How much does the tour cost?	Скóлько стóит экскýрсия? (Skól'ko stó-it ekskúrsiya?)
Do you have a guide who speaks English?	У вас есть экскурсовóд (гид), котóрый говори́т по-англи́йски? (U vas yést' ekskursovód (git), katóruiy gavarít pa-anglíyski?)

We should like to see the new Underground stations.	Мы хотéли бы посмотрéть нóвые стáнции метрó.
	(Mui khatyéli bui pasmatryét' nóvuiye stántsii myetró.)
We should like to go to the theatre/museum, conservatoire.	Мы хотéли бы пойти́ в теáтр (в музéй, в консерватóрию).
	(Mui khatyéli bui paytí f teátr, v muzyéi, f kanservatóriyu.)
I should like to go to the opera. (*Literally*: I should like to listen to an opera.)	Я хотéл бы послýшать óперу. (m.)
	(Ya khatyél bui paslúshat' ópyeru.)
I should like to go to a symphony concert.	Я хотéла бы послýшать симфони́ческий концéрт. (f.)
	(Ya khatyéla bui paslúshat' simfonícheskiy kantsyért.)
We should like to see a ballet.	Мы хотéли бы посмотрéть балéт.
	(Mui khatyéli bui pasmatryét' balyét.)
This is the Exhibition of Soviet Economic Achievements.	Это Вы́ставка Достижéний Нарóдного Хозя́йства. (abbrev.: ВДНХ)
	(Éto Vuístafka Dostizhéniy Naródnavo Khozyáystva.)

SIGHTSEEING

Where can one buy entrance tickets?	Где можно купить входные билеты?
	(Gdye mózhno kupít' fkhadnúiye bilyétui?)
Where is the 'Space' pavilion?	Где павильон «Космос»?
	(Gdye pavil'yón 'Kósmos'?)
Show (me) the sputniks, please.	Покажите, пожалуйста, спутники.
	(Pakazhítye, pazháluysta, sputniki.)
What is that building?	Что это за здание?
	(Shtó éto za zdániye?)
It is a 16th century cathedral (church).	Это собор (церковь) шестнадцатого века.
	(Éto sabór (tsérkof') shyestnádtsatovo vyéka.)
May one take photographs here?	Здесь можно фотографировать?
	(Zydes' mózhno fatagrafírovat'?)
And that is the Moscow University building.	А это здание Московского университета.
	(A éto zdániye Maskófskovo univyersityéta.)
Where can one buy picture postcards?	Где можно купить открытки?
	(Gdye mózhno kupít' otkruítki?)
We should like to buy the 'Moscow' picture-book.	Мы хотели бы купить альбом «Москва».
	(Mui khatyéli bui kupít' al'bóm 'Maskvá'.)

SPEAK, READ, WRITE RUSSIAN

Some—Any

The meaning of these words in Russian is indicated in various ways.

We got (received) some (several) letters.	Мы получи́ли **не́сколько** пи́сем.
	(Mui paluchíli *nyéskol'ko* písyem.)
Give me some (a little) salt, please.	Да́йте, пожа́луйста, **немно́го** со́ли.
	(Dáytye, pazháluysta, *nyemnógo* sóli.)
I saw it in some book.	Я ви́дел э́то в **како́й-то** кни́ге.
	(Ya vídyel éto f *kakói-to* knígye.)

Russian equivalents of 'some' and 'any' are often omitted altogether.

Have you some meat, any meat?	У вас éсть мя́со?
	(U vas yést myása?)
Have you some cheese, any cheese?	У вас éсть сыр?
	(U vast yést' suír?)
Have you some lemons, any lemons?	У вас éсть лимо́ны?
	(U vas yést' limónui?)
Have you some mineral water, any mineral water?	У вас éсть минера́льная вода́?
	(U vas yést' minerál'naya vadá?)
Have you some wine, any wine?	У вас éсть вино́?
	(U vas yést' vinó?)

SOME—ANY

Give me some milk.	Дайте мне молока.
	(Dáytye mnye malaká.)
Show me some new records.	Покажите мне новые пластинки.
	(Pakazhítye mnye nóvuiye plastínki.)
Someone, anyone.	Кто́-то. Кто-нибу́дь.
	(Któ-to. Kto-nibút'.)
Something, anything.	Что́-то. Что-нибу́дь.
	(Shtó-to. Shto-nibút'.)
Sometimes.	Иногда́.
	(Inogdá.)
Somewhere, anywhere.	Где́-то. Где-нибу́дь.
	(Gdyé-to. Gdye-nibút'.)

TENSES

The Present Tense

In Russian there is only one Present Tense, which may correspond to the English 'Present Indefinite' or 'Present Continuous' tenses, for instance:

Do you read English newspapers?	Вы читаете английские газеты?
	(Vui chitáyetye anglíyskiye gazyétui?)
I am reading an English newspaper now.	Я читаю сейчас английскую газету.
	(Ya chitáyu seichás anglíyskuyu gazyétu.)

There are two principal types of conjugation in the Present Tense. The endings of the first type are:

51

я ду́маю	(ya dúmayu)	-ю	I think
он ду́мает	(on dúmayet)	-ет	he thinks
она́ ду́мает	(oná dúmayet)		she thinks
мы ду́маем	(mui dúmayem)	-ем	we think
вы ду́маете	(vui dúmayetye)	-ете	you think
они́ ду́мают	(aní dúmayut)	-ют	they think

This type includes 'знать' (*to know*), 'спра́шивать' (*to ask*), 'отвеча́ть' (*to answer*), 'приглаша́ть' (*to invite*), 'де́лать' (*to make, to do*), 'чита́ть' (*to read*).

Endings of the second type are:

я слы́шу	(ya sluíshu)	-у	I hear
он слы́шит	(on sluíshit)	-ит	he hears
она́ слы́шит	(oná sluíshit)		she hears
мы слы́шим	(mui sluíshim)	-им	we hear
вы слы́шите	(vui sluíshitye)	-ите	you hear
они слы́шат	(aní sluíshat)	-ат	they hear

Some verbs have 'у' and 'ат' instead of 'ю' and 'ят'. See, for instance, 'говори́ть' (*to say, to tell*) and 'люби́ть' (*to like, to love, to prefer*).

A few verbs change the stem consonant when conjugated. Examples: 'ви́деть' (*to see*), 'плати́ть' (*to pay*), 'приноси́ть' (*to bring*).

To Ask

Imperf. Спра́шивать (spráshivat')
Present:

I ask	я спра́шиваю	(ya spráshivayu)
you ask	вы спра́шиваете	(vui spráshivayetye)
they ask	они́ спра́шивают	(aní spráshivayut)

TO ASK

Perf. Спросить (sprasít')
Future:

I will ask	я спрошу́	(ya sprashú)
you will ask	вы спро́сите	(vui sprósitye)
they will ask	они́ спро́сят	(aní sprósyat)

I am asking you.
Я спра́шиваю вас.
(Ya spráshivayu vas.)

I would like to ask where is the nearest post-office.
Я хочу́ спроси́ть, где ближа́йшая по́чта.
(Ya khachú sprasít', gdye blizháyshaya póchta.)

What is he asking us about?
О чём он нас спра́шивает?
(O chóm on nas spráshivayet?)

Ask the interpreter.
Спроси́те у перево́дчика.
(Sprasítye u pyeryevótchika.)

To Give

Imperf. Дава́ть (davát')
Present:

I give	я даю́	(ya dayú)
you give	вы даёте	(vui dayótye)
they give	они́ даю́т	(aní dayút)

Perf. Дать (dat')
Future:

I will give	я дам	(ya dam)
you will give	вы дади́те	(vui dadítye)
he will give	он даст	(on dast)
we will give	мы дади́м	(mui dadím)
they will give	они́ даду́т	(aní dadút)

Past:
- I/he gave — я/он дал (ya/on dal) (m.)
- I/she gave — я/она́ дала́ (ya/oná dalá) (f.)
- we/they gave — мы/они́ да́ли (mui/aní dáli) (pl.)

Imperative:
- Give me — Да́йте мне (Dáytye mnye)
- Give us — Да́йте нам (Dáytye nam)

I am giving you two tickets. Я даю́ вам два биле́та. (Ya dayú vam dva bilyéta.)

Did you give him (the) money? Вы да́ли ему́ де́ньги? (Vui dáli yemú dyén'gi?)

To Hurry

Imperf. Спеши́ть (spyeshít')

Present:
- I am in a hurry — я спешу́ (ya spyeshú)
- we are in a hurry — мы спеши́м (mui spyeshím)
- you are in a hurry — вы спеши́те (vui spyeshítye)
- he is in a hurry — он спеши́т (on spyeshít)
- they are in a hurry — они́ спеша́т (aní spyeshát)

Imperf. Торопи́ться (tarapít'sya)

Present:
- I am in a hurry — я тороплю́сь (ya taraplyús')
- we are in a hurry — мы торо́пимся (mui tarópimsya)
- you are in a hurry — вы торо́питесь (vui tarópityes')

TO HURRY

he is in a hurry	он торо́пится (on taró pitsya)
they are in a hurry	они́ торо́пятся (ani taró pyatsya)
Excuse me, I am in a hurry.	Извини́те, я спешу́/я торо-плю́сь. (Izvinítye, ya spyeshú/ya taraplyús'.)
Are you in a hurry?	Вы спеши́те? Вы торо́питесь? (Vui spyeshítye? Vui tarópityes'?)
Don't be in a hurry.	Не спеши́те. Не торопи́тесь. (Nye spyeshítye. Nye tarapítyes'.)

The Past Tense

In the Past Tense, Russian verbs change only according to gender and number. It is formed by substituting for the final consonant the endings:

-л   for the masculine gender;
-ла for the feminine gender;
-ло for the neuter gender;
-ли for the plural.

Here are some examples with the verb **'посла́ть'** (paslát')—'to send': note that *verbs* in the Past Tense agree with the *subject* in gender and number.

I have sent a letter to England. (A man speaking.)	Я посла́л письмо́ в А́нглию. (m.) (Ya paslál pis'mó v Ángliyu.)

I have sent a letter to France. (A woman speaking.)	Я посла́ла письмо́ во Фра́нцию. (f.) (Ya paslála pís'mo vo Frántsiyu.)
Have you sent the telegram to Kiev? (Addressing one or several persons.)	Вы посла́ли телегра́мму в Ки́ев? (pl.) (Vui paslíli tyelyegrámu f Kíyef?)

The Future Tense

There are two Future Tenses in Russian: the Compound Future and the Simple Future. Both may correspond either to the Future Indefinite or Future Continuous in English.

The Compound Future Tense is formed only from Imperfective verbs (see A SIMPLE VERB and THE VERB). It consists of the future of the verb 'быть'—to be (see TO BE) followed by the infinitive of the verb.

We shall stay at the 'Ukraina' Hotel. (*Literally*: We shall live in the 'Ukraina' hotel.)	Мы бу́дем жить в гости́нице «Украи́на». (Mui búdyem zhit' v gastínitsye 'Ukraína'.)
You will take the medicine twice a day.	Вы бу́дете принима́ть лека́рство два ра́за в де́нь. (Vui búdyetye prinimát' lyekárstva dva razá v dyén'.)
I shall wait for you at the metro entrance.	Я бу́ду ждать вас у вхо́да в метро́. (Ya búdu zhdat' vas u fkhóda v myetró.)

The Simple Future Tense is formed only from Perfective verbs.

THE FUTURE TENSE

Perfective verbs are conjugated in the same way as Imperfective verbs. If a Perfective verb is formed by means of a prefix its conjugation pattern is identical with that of its imperfective counterpart.

Imperf.	я плачу́ (ya plachú)	I am paying, I pay
Perf.	я заплачу́ (ya zaplachú)	I will pay, I will be paying
Imperf.	он ждёт (on zhdyót)	he is waiting
Perf.	он подождёт (on padazhdyót)	he will wait

If Perfective and Imperfective verbs have different suffixes they may belong to different types of conjugation:

Imperf. спра́шивать
        (spráshivat')   to ask   1st conjugation
Perf.   спроси́ть
        (sprasít)   to ask   2nd conjugation
(see TO ASK).

IDIOMS

Some Russian phrases cannot be translated literally into English. You will simply have to memorise them as they are. Here are a few.

How are you (getting on)? or How are things?	Как ва́ши дела́? (Kak váshi dyelá?)
Everything's all right.	Всё в поря́дке. (Vsyó f paryátkye.)
Thank you. Not at all.	Спаси́бо. Не́ за что. (Spasíba. Nyé za shtó.)
At first. At once.	Снача́ла. Сра́зу. (Snachála. Srazú.)

SPEAK, READ, WRITE RUSSIAN

Your health!	За ва́ше здоро́вье!
	(Za váshye zdaróv'ye!)
Bon appetit!	Прия́тного аппети́та!
	(Priyátnavo appyetíta!)
Goodbye!	Всего́ хоро́шего!
(*Literally*: All the best!)	(Vsyevó kharóshevo!)
See you this evening.	До ве́чера.
(*Literally*: Till the evening.)	(Da vyéchera.)
Many happy returns of the day!	С днём рожде́ния!
	(S dnyóm razhdéniya!)

Expressions of Time

Now	Сейча́с (Seichás)
Today	Сего́дня (Syevódnya)
Tomorrow	За́втра (Záftra)
Yesterday	Вчера́ (Fcherá)
Every day	Ка́ждый де́нь (Kázhduiy dén')
In the morning	У́тром (Útrom)
In the afternoon	Днём (Dnyóm)
In the evening	Ве́чером (Vyécherom)
At night	Но́чью (Nóch'yu)
Long ago	Давно́ (Davnó)
Not long ago	Неда́вно (Nyedávno)
Within five days	Че́рез пя́ть дней (Chéryes pyát' dnyéy)
Five days ago	Пя́ть дней тому́ наза́д (Pyát' dnyéy tamú nazát)
This morning	Сего́дня у́тром (Syevódnya útrom)
Yesterday evening	Вчера́ ве́чером (Fcherá vyécherom)
In time, punctually	Во́-время (Vó-vryemya)
At the same time	В то́ же вре́мя (F tó zhe vryémya)

EXPRESSIONS OF TIME

In time (course of)	Со врéменем (Sa vryémyenyem)
Once, twice	Одúн рáз, двá рáза (Adín raz, dva ráza)
The first time/occasion	Пéрвый раз (Pyérvuiy raz)
The next time	В слéдующий раз (F slyéduyushchiy raz)
For the last time	В послéдний раз (F paslyédniy raz)
Several times	Нéсколько раз (Nyéskol'ka raz)
It is time (to go)	Порá иттú (éхать) (Porá ittí/ yékhat')
At first, at once	Сначáла, срáзу (Snachála, srázu)

Time by the Clock

Before reading this, refer to the section on numerals, p. 143

One o'clock.	Час. (Chas.)
Three o'clock.	Три часá. (Tri chasá.)
Seven o'clock.	Семь часóв. (Syem' chasóf.)
Ten past two. (*Literally*: Ten minutes of the third (hour).)	Дéсять минýт трéтьего. (Dyésyat' minút tryét'yevo.)
Ten past two. (*Literally*: Two hours ten minutes.)	Два часá дéсять минýт. (Dva chasá dyésyat' minút.)
Ten to two. (*Literally*: Ten minutes short of two.)	Без десятú минýт двá. (Byez dyesyatí minút dvá.)
Half past seven. (*Literally*: Half past of the eighth (hour).)	Половúна восьмóго. (Palavína vas'móvo.)

SPEAK, READ, WRITE RUSSIAN

Half past seven. (*Literally*: Seven hours 30 minutes.)	Сéмь часóв трúдцать минýт. (Syém' chasóf tríttsat' minút.)
A quarter past five.	Чéтверть шестóго. (Chétvyert' shestóvo.)
A quarter past five.	Пять часóв пятнáдцать минýт. (Pyát' chasóf pyatnáttsat' minút.)
A quarter to five.	Без чéтверти пять. (Byez chétvyerti pyát'.)
A quarter to five.	Без пятнáдцати (минýт) пять. (Byez pyatnáttsati (minút) pyát'.)
What time is it? (*Literally*: What hour is it? What is the time?)	Котóрый час? Скóлько врéмени? (Katóruiy chas? Skól'ko vryémeni?)
It's now four p.m. (*Literally*: ... in the afternoon.)	Сейчáс четы́ре часá дня. (Seichás chetuírye chasá dnyá.)
It's now five p.m. (*Literally*: ... in the evening.)	Сейчáс пять часóв вéчера. (Seichás pyát' chasóf vyéchera.)
At what hour do we meet?	В котóром часý мы встречáемся? (F katórom chasú mui fstryecháyemsya?)

TIME BY THE CLOCK

We shall meet at 11 a.m. (*Literally*: . . . in the morning.)	Мы встреча́емся в оди́ннадцать утра́. (Mui fstryecháyemsya v adínnattsat' utrá.)
When do you leave? (*Literally*: . . . go away.)	Когда́ вы уезжа́ете? (Kagdá vui uyezháyetye?)
We are leaving on Sunday at three o'clock.	Мы уезжа́ем в воскресе́нье в три часа́. (Mui uyezháyem v vaskryesyén'ye f trí chasá.)

In ordinary conversation time is denoted by numbers from 1 to 12. In official language, however, the range is from 0 to 24. So you may hear a Radio Moscow announcer say: 'Моско́вское вре́мя ноль часо́в' (Maskófskoye vryémya nól' chasóf). Colloquially this corresponds to: 'Двена́дцать часо́в но́чи' (Dvyenáttsat' chasóf nóchi)—Twelve at night, or to и́ли (íli) «По́лночь» (Pólnoch')—Midnight.

Notices of shop trading hours look like this:

This shop is open from 1100 to 1900 hours. (*Literally*: . . . works from . . .)	Магази́н рабо́тает с 11 до 19 часо́в. (Magazín rabótayet s adínnattsati do dyevyatnáttsati chasóf.)
On Mondays from 1100 to 1700 hours.	В понеде́льник с 11 до 17 часо́в. (F panyedyél'nik s adínnattsati do syemnáttsati chasóf.)

VERBS OF MOVEMENT

Russian verbs of movement have a number of special features. Here are the more important:

1. They show the exact manner of movement: whether it is on foot, by some conveyance, plane, ship, etc. The English verb 'to go' can be translated into Russian by:

идти́ (ittí) imperf. to go on foot, to walk
éхать (yékhat') imperf. to go in a vehicle
летáть (lyetát') imperf. to go by aeroplane, to fly
плы́ть (pluit') imperf. to go by ship, to sail

It is worth learning the conjugation of the most common verbs of movement— 'идти́' and 'éхать'.

Imperf. **Идти́** (ittí)
Present:

я иду́	(ya idú)	I am going (on foot)
вы идёте	(vui idyótye)	you are going (on foot)
он идёт	(on idyót)	he is going (on foot)
мы идём	(mui idyóm)	we are going (on foot)
они́ иду́т	(aní idút)	they are going (on foot)

Perf. **Пойти́** (paytí)
Future:

я пойду́	(ya paydú)	I will go
вы пойдёте	(vui paydyótye)	you will go
он пойдёт	(on paydyót)	he will go
мы пойдём	(mui paydyóm)	we will go
они́ пойду́т	(aní paidút)	they will go

Imperf. **Éхать** (yékhat')
Present:

я éду	(ya yédu)	I am going (in a car)
вы éдете	(vui yédyetye)	you are going (in a car)

VERBS OF MOVEMENT

он е́дет	(on yédyet)	he is going (in a car)
мы е́дем	(mui yédyem)	we are going (in a car)
они́ е́дут	(aní yédut)	they are going (in a car)

Perf. Пое́хать (payékhat')
Future:

я пое́ду	(ya payédu)	I will go (in a car)
вы пое́дете	(vui payédyetye)	you will go (in a car)
он пое́дет	(on payédyet)	he will go (in a car)
мы пое́дем	(mui payédyem)	we will go (in a car)
они́ пое́дут	(aní payédut)	they will go (in a car)

Examples

Where are you going now? (on foot)	Куда́ вы сейча́с идёте? (Kudá vui seichás idyótye?)
I am going to the barber's/hairdresser's.	Я иду́ в парикма́херскую. (Ya idú f parikmákhyerskuyu.)
Where will you go tomorrow? (by conveyance)	Куда́ вы пое́дете за́втра? (Kudá vui payédyetye záftra?)
Tomorrow we'll go to Leningrad.	За́втра мы пое́дем в Ленингра́д. (Záftra mui payédyem v Lyeningrát.)
Are you going by train?	Вы е́дете по́ездом? (Vui yédyetye póyezdom?)
We'll go by bus.	Мы пое́дем в авто́бусе. (Mui payédyem v aftóbusye.)

2. Russian verbs of movement also show whether the action is habitual or momentary. Compare:

| ходи́ть | (khadít') | to go on foot (habitually, usually) |
| идти́ | (ittí) | to go on foot (at a given moment) |

ездить (yézdit') to go in a vehicle (habitually)
ехать (yékhat') to go in a vehicle (at a given moment)

Conjugation of **'ходи́ть'** (khadít'):

Present:

я хожу́	(ya khazhú)	I go
вы хо́дите	(vui khóditye)	you go
он хо́дит	(on khódit)	he goes
мы хо́дим	(mui khódim)	we go
они́ хо́дят	(aní khódyat)	they go

Past:

я/он ходи́л	(ya/on khadíl)	I/he went	(m.)
я/она́ ходи́ла	(ya/oná khadíla)	I/she went	(f.)
мы/вы ходи́ли	(mui/vui khadíli)	we/you went	(pl.)

'Ходи́л', etc. (the Past of 'ходи́ть') and 'е́здил', etc. (the Past of 'е́здить') are frequently used for the Past Tense forms of 'идти́' and 'е́хать'.

We often go to the cinema in the evening.	Ве́чером мы ча́сто хо́дим в кино́. (Vyécherom mui chásto khódim f kinó.)
In the summer we often went to the swimming pool.	Ле́том мы ча́сто ходи́ли в бассе́йн. (Lyétom mui chásto khadíli v bassyéyn.)
We are now going to the cinema.	Сейча́с мы идём в кино́. (Seichás mui idyóm f kinó.)
We went to the cinema yesterday.	Мы ходи́ли в кино́ вчера́. (Mui khadíli f kinó fcherá.)
The tourists are going to Leningrad.	Тури́сты е́дут в Ленингра́д. (Turístui yédut v Lyeningrát.)

VERBS OF MOVEMENT

They went to Leningrad in the winter. Они́ е́здили в Ленингра́д зимо́й.
(Aní yézdili v Lyeningrát zimói.)

3. Russian verbs of movement take prefixes indicating direction. Here we give a few of them.

The prefix 'в' adds 'into' to the meaning of movement.

входи́ть (fkhadít'), Imperf.
    to enter, to come in (on foot)
войти́ (vaytí), Perf.
    to enter, to come in (on foot)
въе́хать (vyékhat'), Perf.
    to enter, to come in (by vehicle)

'При' adds the meaning of 'toward', 'arriving', to movement.

прие́хать (priyékhat'), Perf.
    to come, to arrive (in a vehicle)
приезжа́ть (priyezhát'), Imperf.
    to come, to arrive (in a vehicle)
приходи́ть (prikhadít'), Imperf.
    to come, to arrive, (on foot)
прийти́ (priytí), Perf.
    to come, to arrive (on foot)

The prefix 'у' adds the meaning of 'motion away from.'

уе́хать (uyékhat'), Perf.
    to depart, leave go away (in a vehicle)
уезжа́ть (uyezhát'), Imperf.
    to depart, leave, go away (in a vehicle)
уйти́ (uytí), Perf.
    to depart, leave, go away (on foot)

SPEAK, READ, WRITE RUSSIAN

уходи́ть (ukhadít'), Imperf.
to depart, leave, go away (on foot)

May I come in?	Мо́жно войти́?
	(Mózhno vaytí?)
Come in, please.	Входи́те, пожа́луйста.
	(Fkhadítye, pazháluysta.)
When will you come to visit us?	Когда́ вы прие́дете к нам в го́сти?
(*Literally*: When will you come to us as guests?)	(Kagdá vui priyédyetye k nam v gósti?)
The tourists from Canada arrive in Moscow today.	Тури́сты из Кана́ды приезжа́ют сего́дня в Москву́.
	(Turístui iz Kanádui priyezháyut syevódnya v Maskvú.)
Come to (see) us again.	Приходи́те к нам ещё раз.
	(Prikhadítye k nam yeshchó raz.)
We will certainly come here again.	Мы обяза́тельно придём сюда́ ещё раз.
	(Mui abyezátel'no pridyóm syudá yeshchó raz.)
We are leaving today at 3 p.m.	Мы уезжа́ем сего́дня в три часа́ дня.
	(Mui uyezháyem syevódnya f tri chasá dnya.)
My friends have already left.	Мои́ друзья́ уже́ уе́хали.
	(Maí druz'yá uzhé uyékhali.)
Are you leaving already?	Вы уже́ ухо́дите?
	(Vui uzhé ukhóditye?)

VERBS OF MOVEMENT

We must leave now, but we shall be back in an hour.
Сейча́с мы должны́ уйти́, но че́рез час мы вернёмся.
(Seichás mui dalzhnuí uytí, no chéryez chas mui vyernyómsya.)

Travelling

Are you going to Kiev today?
Вы е́дете сего́дня в Ки́ев?
(Vui yédyetye syevódnya f Kíyef?)

Will you go by plane?
Вы полети́те самолётом?
(Vui palyetítye samolyótom?)

I should like to go by train.
Я хоте́л бы пое́хать в по́езде.
(Ya khatyél bui payékhat' v póyezde.)

The train leaves in forty minutes.
По́езд отхо́дит че́рез со́рок мину́т.
(Póyezd atkhódit chéryez sórok minút.)

Is it far to the station?
До вокза́ла далеко́?
(Do vagzála dalyekó?)

Is it possible to walk there?
Мо́жно дойти́ туда́ пешко́м?
(Mózhno daytí tudá pyeshkóm?)

The station is a long way away.
(*Literally*: To the station is far.)
До вокза́ла далеко́.
(Da vagzála dalyekó.)

(It's) about three kilometres.
О́коло трёх киломе́тров.
(Ókalo tryókh kilomyétrof.)

67

It would be better to take a taxi.	Лу́чше взя́ть такси́. (Lútshe vzyát' taksí.)
I must go immediately.	Я до́лжен е́хать сейча́с же. (Ya dólzhen yékhat' seichás zhe.)
Call me a taxi, please.	Вы́зовите мне такси́, пожа́луйста. (Vuízovitye mnye taksí, pazháluysta.)
Where do you want to go? (*Literally*: Where to for you?)	Куда́ вам? (Kudá vam?)
To the Kiev station, please.	На Ки́евский вокза́л пожа́луйста. (Na Kíyefskiy vagzál, pazháluysta.)
We shall be late.	Мы опа́здываем. (Mui apázduivayem.)
Don't worry. You'll get there in time.	Не беспоко́йтесь. Вы успе́ете. (Nye byespakóytyes'. Vui uspyéyetye.)
How much do I owe?	Ско́лько я до́лжен? (Skól'ko ya dólzhen?)
Forty copeks.	Со́рок копе́ек. (Sórok kapéyek.)
Where is the booking-office?	Где ка́сса? (Gdye kássa?)
The booking-office is over there, in the next hall. (*Literally*: ... the other hall.)	Ка́сса вон та́м, в друго́м за́ле. (Kássa von tám, v drugóm zálye.)

TRAVELLING

Two tickets to Kiev, please.	Два билéта до Кúева, пожáлуйста.
	(Dvá bilyéta da Kíyeva, pazháluysta.)
All tickets have been sold.	Всé билéты прóданы.
	(Vsye bilyétui pródanui.)
Our tickets were ordered five days ago.	Нáши билéты закáзаны пять днéй назáд.
	(Náshi bilyétui zakázanui pyát' dnyéi nazád.)
I have a lot of luggage.	У меня́ мнóго багажá.
	(U myenyá mnógo bagazhá.)
Porter, are you free?	Носи́льщик, вы свобóдны?
	(Nasíl'shchik, vui svabódnui?)
(Take it) to the sixth carriage, please.	В шестóй вагóн, пожáлуйста.
	(F shestói vagón, pazháluysta.)
Where are you going?	Кудá вы éдете?
	(Kudá vui yédyetye?)
We are going to Kiev.	Мы éдем в Кúев.
	(Mui yédyem f Kíyef.)
How long does it take to get to Kiev? (*Literally*: How many hours does the train go to Kiev?)	Скóлько часóв идёт пóезд до Кúева?
	(Skól'ko chasóf idyót póyest da Kíyeva?)
There is a restaurant-car on the train.	В пóезде éсть вагóн-ресторáн.
	(F póyezdye yést' vagón-restarán.)

69

SPEAK, READ, WRITE RUSSIAN

Happy journey!   Счастливого пути!
(Shchaslívavo putí!)

To Understand

Imperf. Понима́ть (panimát')

Present:
I understand	я понима́ю	(ya panimáyu)
you understand	вы понима́ете	(vui panimáyetye)
they understand	они́ понима́ют	(aní panimáyut)

Future:
- I shall understand   я бу́ду понима́ть
  (ya búdu panimát')
- you will understand   вы бу́дете понима́ть
  (vui búdyetye panimát')
- they will understand   они́ бу́дут понима́ть
  (aní búdut panimát')

Perf. Поня́ть (panyát')

Future:
I will understand	я пойму́	(ya paimú)
you will understand	вы поймёте	(vui paimyótye)
they will understand	они́ пойму́т	(aní paimút)

Past:
- I/he understood   я/он по́нял (m.)
  (ya/on pónyal)
- I/she understood   я/она́ поняла́ (f.)
  (ya/oná ponyalá)
- you/we understood   вы/мы по́няли (pl.)
  (vui/mui pónyali)

Do you understand me?   Вы меня́ понима́ете?
(Vui myenyá panimáyetye?)

TO UNDERSTAND

Speak more slowly, please. I don't understand Russian very well.

Говори́те, пожа́луйста, ме́дленее, я пло́хо понима́ю по-ру́сски.

(Gavarítye, pazháluysta, myédlyenneye, ya plókho panimáyu pa-rússki.)

We did not understand what you said.

Мы не по́няли, что́ вы сказа́ли.

(Mui nye pónyali, shtó vui skazáli.)

You may speak Russian, I will understand you.

Вы мо́жете говори́ть по-ру́сски, я вас пойму́.

(Vui mózhetye gavarít' pa-rússki, ya vas paimú.)

If you listen to Russian records you will understand Russian well.

Éсли вы бу́дете слу́шать ру́сские пласти́нки, вы бу́дете хорошо́ понима́ть по-ру́сски.

(Yésli vui búdyetye slúshat' rússkiye plastínki, vui búdyetye kharashó panimát' pa-rússki.)

Days of the Week

Monday	понеде́льник	(m.)	(panyedyél'nik)
Tuesday	вто́рник	(m.)	(ftórnik)
Wednesday	среда́	(f.)	(sryedá)
Thursday	четве́рг	(m.)	(chetvyérg)
Friday	пя́тница	(f.)	(pyátnitsa)
Saturday	суббо́та	(f.)	(subóta)
Sunday	воскресе́нье	(n.)	(vaskryesyén'ye)

SPEAK, READ, WRITE RUSSIAN

What day is it today?	Какóй сегóдня дéнь?
	(Kakói syevódnya dyén'?)
Today is Wednesday (Thursday, Tuesday).	Сегóдня средá (четвéрг, втóрник).
	(Syevódnya sryedá (chetvyérg, ftórnik).)
When do you wish to go to Leningrad?	Когдá вы хотúте поéхать в Ленингрáд?
	(Kagdá vui khatítye payékhat' v Lyeningrát?)
We should like to go to Leningrad on Wednesday/Thursday/Tuesday.	Мы хотéли бы поéхать в Ленингрáд в срéду/в четвéрг/во втóрник.
	(Mui khatyéli bui payékhat' v Lyeningrát f sryédu/f chetvyérg/va ftórnik.)
We don't work on Saturday or on Sunday.	В суббóту и в воскресéнье мы не рабóтаем.
(*Literally*: Saturday and ...)	(F subbótu i v vaskryesyén'ye mui nye rabótayem.)

Months
(all masculine; see NOUNS)

January	янвáрь	(yanvár')
February	феврáль	(fevrál')
March	мáрт	(márt)
April	апрéль	(apryél')
May	май	(máy)
June	иóнь	(iyún')
July	иóль	(iyúl')
August	áвгуст	(ávgust)

MONTHS

September	сентя́брь	(syentyábr')
October	октя́брь	(aktyábr')
November	ноя́брь	(nayábr')
December	декáбрь	(dyekábr')

What month are we in now?
(*Literally*: . . . is it now?)

Какóй сейчáс мéсяц?
(Kakói seichás myésyats?)

It is now August/September.

Сейчáс áвгуст/сентя́брь.
(Seichás ávgust/syentyábr'.)

In which month will you be coming to Moscow?

В какóм мéсяце вы приéдете в Москвý?
(F kakóm myésyatsye vui priyédyetye v Maskvú?)

I shall come to Moscow in August/in September.

Я приéду в Москвý в áвгусте/в сентябрé.
(Ya priyédu v Maskvú v ávgustye/v syentyabryé.)

Seasons

spring	веснá	(f.)	(vyesná)
summer	лéто	(n.)	(lyéto)
autumn	óсень	(f.)	(ósyen')
winter	зимá	(f.)	(zimá)
in spring	веснóй		(vyesnói)
in summer	лéтом		(lyétom)
in autumn	óсенью		(ósyen'yu)
in winter	зимóй		(zimói)

POSSESSION

There are several ways in Russian to express the idea that a thing (or things) belongs (or belong) to somebody.

SPEAK, READ, WRITE RUSSIAN

One is by using possessive pronouns.

Here is my luggage.	Вóт мóй багáж (Vót mói bagázh)
Where is your passport?	Гдé вáш паспорт? (Gdyé vásh pásport?)
Give (us) our key.	Дáйте наш клю́ч. (Dáytye nash klyúch.)
This suitcase is mine.	Э́тот чемодáн мóй. (Étot chemadán mói.)
These tickets are yours.	Э́ти билéты вáши. (Éti bilyétui váshi.)

The possessive pronouns мой, наш, ваш, like all adjectives, agree with the noun in gender, number and case. The possessives which correspond to the pronouns он, онá, онó and они́ have only one form (егó, её, их).

my	мóй (m.) (mói)	мóй пáспорт (mói pásport)	my passport
my	моя́ (f.) (mayá)	моя́ кóмната (mayá kómnata)	my room
my	моё (n.) (mayó)	моё письмó (mayó pis'mó)	my letter
my	мой (pl.) (maí)	мой друзья́ (maí druz'yá)	my friends
your	твóй (m.) (tvói)	твóй багáж (tvói bagázh)	your luggage
your	твоя́ (f.) (tvayá)	твоя́ су́мка (tvayá súmka)	your bag
your	твоё (n.) (tvayó)	твоё и́мя (tvayó ímya)	your name
your	твой (pl.) (tvaí)	твой значки́ (tvaí znachkí)	your badges

POSSESSION

The pronoun 'твой' etc. is in the 2nd person singular (see note regarding 2nd person singular on p. 23); it corresponds to the pronoun 'ты' (tui) (see PRONOUNS).

her	её (m., f., n., pl.) (yeyó)	её билéт (yeyó bilyét)	her ticket
		её пластинка (yeyó plastínka)	her record
		её письмó (yeyó pis'mó)	her letter
		её откры́тки (yeyó atkruítki)	her postcards
his	егó (m., f., n., pl.) (yevó)	егó ключ (yevó kluch)	his key
		егó машина (yevó mashína)	his car
		егó сигарéты (yevó sigaryétui)	his cigarettes

Note that in the possessive pronoun 'егó' (his), as well as in a few other words (such as 'сегóдня', today) and in possessive suffixes, the consonant 'г' is pronounced as 'v': 'егó'—'yevó' (his).

our	наш (m.) (nash)	наш автóбус (násh aftóbus)	our bus
our	нáша (f.) (násha)	нáша экскýрсия (násha ekskúrsiya)	our excursion
our	нáше (n.) (náshe)	нáше врéмя (náshe vryémya)	our time
our	нáши (pl.) (náshi)	нáши машины (náshi mashínui)	our cars
your	ваш (m.) (vásh)	ваш зáвтрак (vásh záftrak)	your breakfast

your	ва́ша (f.) (vásha)	ва́ша ча́шка (vásha cháshka)	your cup
your	ва́ше (n.) (váshe)	ва́ше вино́ (váshe vinó)	your wine
your	ва́ши (pl.) (váshi)	ва́ши де́ньги (váshi dyén'gi)	your money
their	их (m., f., n., pl.) (ikh)	их го́род (ikh górot)	their town
		их гости́ница (ikh gastínitsa)	their hotel
		их расписа́ние (ikh raspisániye)	their timetable
		их авто́бусы (ikh aftóbusui)	their buses

Possession can also be expressed:

(*a*) by the *Genitive* case of the noun.

This is John's dictionary.	Э́то слова́рь **Джо́на**. (Éto slavár' Dzhóna.)
Where is the interpreter's seat?	Где ме́сто **перево́дчика**? Gdye myésto pyeryevódchika?

(*b*) In phrases containing 'to have', translated by the use of the preposition **'y'** and the verb **'быть'**, e.g.

I have the dictionary.	У меня́ **есть** слова́рь. (U myenyá yést' slovár'.)
Have you the ticket?	У вас **есть** биле́т? (U vas yést' bilyét?)
We have money.	У нас **есть** де́ньги. (U nas yést' dyén'gi.)
He has a car.	У него́ **есть** маши́на. (U nyevó yést' mashína.)

POSSESSION

She has cigarettes.	У неё **есть** сигареты.
	(U nyeyó yést' sigaryétui.)
They have (postage) stamps.	У них **есть** марки.
	(U nikh yést' márki.)

In Russian usage the word 'postage' is often implied, without being specifically stated.

I had a ticket.	У меня **был** билет.
	(U myenyá buil bilyét.)
Had you tickets?	У вас **были** билеты?
	(U vas buíli bilyétui?)

To Have

According to the dictionary, the Russian translation of '*to have*' is 'иметь' (imyét')—я имею (ya imyéyu), вы имеете (vui imyéyetye), они имеют (aní imyéyut), etc.

However, in Russian this verb is used less frequently than 'to have' is used in English. Compare:

We had a cup of coffee.	Мы выпили чашку кофе.
(*Literally*: We drank . . .)	(Mui vuípili cháshku kófye.)
I had a letter.	Я получил письмо.
(*Literally*: I received . . .)	(Ya paluchíl pis'mó.)

The following phrases are used to denote possession:

I have	у меня есть	(u myenyá yést')
you have	у вас есть	(u vas yést')
we have	у нас есть	(u nas yést')
he has	у него есть	(u nyevó yést')
she has	у неё есть	(u nyeyó yést')
they have	у них есть	(u nikh yést')

We had a timetable.	У нас бы́ло расписа́ние. (U nas buílo raspisániye.)
He will have a car.	У него́ бу́дет маши́на. (U nyevó búdyet mashína.)
She will have time.	У неё бу́дет вре́мя. (U nyeyó búdyet vryémya.)
They will have money.	У них бу́дут де́ньги. (U nikh búdut dyén'gi.)

In the Present Tense the verb 'есть' is sometimes omitted altogether.

I have many records	У меня́ мно́го пласти́нок. (U myenyá mnógo plastínak.)
He has good books.	У него́ хоро́шие кни́ги. (U nyevó kharóshiye knígi.)

On the use of the negative in sentences conveying the idea of possession see NEGATION.

The verb 'есть' emphasises possession.

Have you tickets?	У вас есть биле́ты? (U vas yést' bilyétui?)
I have many friends.	У меня́ мно́го друзе́й. (U myenyá mnógo druz'yéi.)

In the Past Tense 'есть' is replaced by был, была́, бы́ло, бы́ли, depending on the gender and number of the noun following the verb. In the Future Tense either 'бу́дет' or 'бу́дут', depending on the number of the noun, is used.

He had a good car.	У него́ была́ хоро́шая маши́на. (U nyevó builá kharóshaya mashína.)

TO HAVE

We had one ticket.	У нас бы́л оди́н биле́т.
	(U nas buíl adín bilyét.)
She had good books.	У неё бы́ли хоро́шие кни́ги.
	(U nyeyó buíli kharóshiye knígi.)
Will you have time to spare tomorrow?	У вас за́втра бу́дет свобо́дное вре́мя?
	(U vas záftra búdyet svabódnoye vryémya?)
We shall have new records tomorrow.	У нас за́втра бу́дут но́вые пласти́нки.
	(U nas záftra búdut nóvuiye plastínki.)

Health
(Note the use of 'себя', syebyá—oneself.)

How are you?	Ка́к вы себя́ чу́вствуете?
(*Literally*: How do you yourself feel?)	(Kák vui syebyá chústvuyetye?)
Very well, thank you.	О́чень хорошо́, спаси́бо.
	(Óchen' kharashó, spasíbo.)
How is your husband?	Ка́к чу́вствует себя́ ваш му́ж?
	(Kak chústvuyet syebyá vash múzh?)
He is not too well.	Он чу́вствует себя́ нева́жно.
	(On chústvuyet syebyá nyevázhno.)
Where does it hurt?	Что́ у ва́с боли́т?
(*Literally*: What hurts you?)	(Shtó u vás balít?)
I have a headache.	**У меня́ боли́т** голова́.
	(U myenyá balít galavá.)

I have a stomach-ache.	У меня́ боли́т желу́док. (zhelúdok)
I have a sore throat.	У меня́ боли́т го́рло. (górlo)
I have a toothache.	У меня́ боли́т зу́б. (zúp)
My leg hurts.	У меня́ боли́т нога́. (nogá)
My hand hurts.	У меня́ боли́т рука́. (ruká)
I have caught a cold.	Я простуди́лся. (Ya prastudílsya.)
Please call the doctor.	Вы́зовите, пожа́луйста, врача́. (Vuízavitye, pazháluysta, vrachá.)
Will I have to have an operation? (*Literally*: Will they perform an operation on me?)	Мне́ бу́дут де́лать опера́цию? (Mnyé búdut dyélat' apyerátsiyu?)
Will I have to go into hospital?	Я до́лжен ле́чь в больни́цу? (Ya dólzhen lyéch' v bal'nítsu?)
Where is the chemist's (round) here?	Где́ здесь апте́ка? (Gdyé zdyés' aptyéka?)
Here is (your) medicine. Take it three times a day.	Вот лека́рство. Принима́йте его́ три раза́ в де́нь. (Vót lyekárstvo. Primimáytye yevó tri razá v dyén'.)
How much should I pay the doctor?	Ско́лько я до́лжен заплати́ть врачу́? (Skól'ko ya dólzhen zaplatít' vrachú?)
There is nothing to pay.	Не ну́жно ничего́ плати́ть. (Nye núzhno nichevó platít'.)

HEALTH

I am quite well now.	Сейча́с я совсе́м здоро́в (m.)/здоро́ва (f.).
	(Seichás ya safsyém zdaróf/zdaróva.)
Are you satisfied with the medical service?	Вы дово́льны медици́нским обслу́живанием?
	(Vui davól'nui myeditsínskim apslúzhivaniyem?)

Post Office

Where is the post office (here)?	Где́ здесь по́чта?
	(Gdyé zdyes' póchta?)
The post office is in the hotel, on the ground floor.	По́чта в гости́нице, на пе́рвом этаже́.
	(Póchta v gastínitse, na pyérvom etazhyé.)
Have you any picture postcards of the Kremlin?	У вас е́сть откры́тки с ви́дами Кремля́?
(*Literally*: ... postcards with views of the Kremlin.)	(U vas yést' atkruítki s vídami Kryemlyá?)
I want to send a letter to England.	Я хочу́ посла́ть письмо́ в А́нглию.
	(Ya khachú paslát' pis'mó v Ángliyu.)
How much does it cost to send a letter abroad?	Ско́лько сто́ит посла́ть письмо́ заграни́цу?
	(Skól'ko stoít paslát' pis'mó zagranítsu?)
Give (me some) stamps, please.	Да́йте, пожа́луйста, ма́рки.
	(Dáytye, pazháluysta, márki.)

81

I want to send a telegram.	Я хочу послать телеграмму. (Ya khachú paslát' tyelyegrámmu.)
Fill in this form.	Заполните этот бланк. (Zapólnitye étot blánk.)
May I send this parcel?	Можно послать эту посылку? (Mózhno paslát' étu pasuílku?)

Telephone

Where can I telephone?	Где можно позвонить по телефону? (Gdyé mózhno pazvanít' po telefónu?)
There is a telephone here.	Здесь есть телефон. (Zdyés' yést' telefón.)
There is no telephone here. The telephone is downstairs. (*Literally*: below.)	Здесь телефона нет. Телефон внизу. (Zdyés' telefóna nyét. Telefón vnizú.)
I want to ring London.	Я хочу позвонить в Лондон. (Ya khachú pazvanít' v Lóndon.)
The number is engaged.	Номер занят. (Nómyer zányat.)
The number does not answer.	Номер не отвечает. (Nómyer nye atvyecháyet.)
Have you a telephone?	У вас есть телефон? (U vas yést' telefón?)

TELEPHONE

Yes, (I have). Write down the number please.	Да. Пожáлуйста запишúте нóмер. (Da. Pazháluysta zapishítye nómyer.)
My telephone number is 28-30-45.	Мóй телефóн двáдцать вóсемь—трúдцать—сóрок пять. (Mói telefón dváttsat' vósyem'—tríttsat'—sórok pyat'.)
Hello! (*Literally*: I am listening, or Yes.)	Аллó! Я слýшаю/Да. (Alló! Ya slúshayu/Da.)
Please may I speak to Petrov? (*Literally*: Please ask Petrov (to come to the phone).)	Попросúте, пожáлуйста, Петрóва? (Paprosítye, pazháluysta, Pyetróva?)
Petrov is not here just now.	Петрóва сейчáс нéт. (Pyetróva seichás nyét.)
He will be (here) in an hour.	Он бýдет чéрез чáс. (On búdyet chéryez chás.)
Would you like to leave a message? (*Literally*: What (message) to give him?)	Чтó емý передáть? (Shtó yemú peredát'?)
Please tell him John MacPherson rang.	Скажúте, пожáлуйста, чтó звонúл Джóн Макфéрсон. (Skazhítye, pazháluysta, shtó zvaníl Dzhón MacFyérson.)

To Want—To Wish

Imperf. Хотéть (khatyét')

Present:

I want	я хочý	(ya khachú)
you want	вы хотите	(vui khatítye)
he wants	он хóчет	(on khóchyet)
we want	мы хотим	(mui khatím)
they want	они хотя́т	(aní khatyát)

Past:

I/he wanted   я/он хотéл (m.)
(ya/on khatyél)

I/she wanted   я/онá хотéла (f.)
(ya/oná khatyéla)

we/you wanted   мы/вы хотéли (pl.)
(mui/vui khatyéli)

I am hungry (thirsty, sleepy.) (*Literally*: I want to eat, etc.)	Я хочý есть (пить, спать). (Ya khachú yést' (pít', spát').)
I should like a glass of cold water.	Я хотéл бы стакáн холóдной воды́. (Ya khatyél bui stakán khalódnoi vaduí.)
What do you want to do?	Что вы хотите дéлать? (Shtó vui khatítye dyélat'?)
We should like to see a modern Soviet play.	Мы хотим посмотрéть совремéнную совéтскую пьéсу. (Mui khatím pasmatryét' savryemyénnuyu savyétskuyu p'yésu.)

TO WANT—TO WISH

He wants to ring London.	Он хо́чет позвони́ть в Ло́ндон. (On khóchet pazvanít' v Lóndon.)
We should like to buy a good camera.	Мы хоте́ли бы купи́ть хоро́ший фо́то-аппара́т. (Mui khatyéli bui kupít' kharóshiy phóto-apparát.)
On Sunday I wanted (f.) to go to the 'Souvenirs' shop, but it was closed.	В воскресе́нье я хоте́ла пойти́ в магази́н «Сувени́ры», но он был закры́т. (V vaskryesyén'ye ya khatyéla paytí v magazín 'Suvyenírui', no on buil zakrúit.)
If you want to buy souvenirs, you can go to the shop today.	Éсли вы хоти́те купи́ть сувени́ры вы мо́жете пойти́ в магази́н сего́дня. (Yésli vui khatítye kupít' suvyenírui vui mózhetye paytí v magazín syevódnya.)

The Weather

What is the weather like now?	Кака́я сейчас пого́да? (Kakáya seichás pagóda?)
The weather is fine.	Пого́да хоро́шая. (Pagóda kharóshaya.)
It's bad weather.	Пого́да плоха́я. (Pagóda plakháya.)
What do you think of the weather?	Что́ вы ду́маете о пого́де? (Shtó vui dúmayetye o pagódye?)

It's cold.	Хо́лодно. (Khóladno.)
It is warm.	Тепло́. (Tyepló.)
It is hot.	Жа́рко. (Zhárko.)
It is raining/snowing.	Идёт до́ждь/сне́г. (Idyót dósht'/snyék.)
The wind is strong.	Си́льный ве́тер. (Síl'nuiy vyétyer.)
What was the weather like yesterday?	Кака́я пого́да была́ вчера́? (Kakáya pagóda builá fcherá?)
It was cold/warm yesterday.	Вчера́ бы́ло хо́лодно/тепло́. (Fcherá buílo khólodno/tyepló.)
Yesterday it was not very hot.	Вчера́ бы́ло не о́чень жа́рко. (Fcherá buílo nye óchen' zhárko.)
It was raining/snowing.	Шёл до́ждь/сне́г. (Shól dósht'/snyék.)
The wind was strong.	Ве́тер был си́льный. (Vyétyer buil síl'nuiy.)
It was not windy in the morning. (*Literally*: In the morning there was no wind.)	У́тром ве́тра не́ бы́ло. (Útrom vyétra nyé buílo.)
What will the weather be like tomorrow?	Кака́я пого́да бу́дет за́втра? (Kakáya pagóda búdyet záftra?)
One must listen to the weather forecast on the radio.	На́до послу́шать сво́дку пого́ды по ра́дио. (Nádo paslúshat' svótku pagódui po rádio.)

THE WEATHER

Look at the weather forecast in the newspaper.	Посмотри́те сво́дку пого́ды в газе́те.
	(Pasmatrítye svótku pagódui v gazyétye.)
It will be cold/warm tomorrow.	За́втра бу́дет хо́лодно/тепло́.
	(Záftra búdyet khóladno/tyepló.)
It will not rain.	Дождя́ не бу́дет.
	(Dazhdyá nye búdyet.)
If it rains we shall stay at home.	Е́сли бу́дет до́ждь, мы оста́немся до́ма.
	(Yésli búdyet dósht', mui astányemsya dóma.)
I/we must take an umbrella.	Ну́жно взять зо́нтик.
	(Núzhno vzyát' zóntik.)
What is the temperature today?	Кака́я сего́дня температу́ра?
	(Kakáya syevódnya tempyeratúra?)
It is 20°C (below) now. (*Literally*: ... (of frost) ...)	Сейча́с два́дцать гра́дусов (моро́за).
	(Seichás dváttsat' grádusof (maróza).)
It is now 10°C (above). (*Literally*: of heat.)	Сейча́с де́сять гра́дусов (тепла́).
	(Seichás dyésyat' grádusof (tyeplá).)
Aren't you cold?	Вам не хо́лодно?
	(Vám nye khóladno?)
I am cold/warm.	Мне хо́лодно/тепло́.
	(Mnyé khóladno/tyepló.)

It's very hot here. The window ought to be opened. (*Literally*: ... It's necessary, etc.)	Здесь о́чень жа́рко. На́до откры́ть окно́. (Zdyés' óchen' zhárko. Nádo atkrúit' aknó.)
Put something warm on, or you will be cold.	Наде́ньте что́-нибу́дь тёплое, а то́ вам бу́дет хо́лодно. (Nadyén'tye shtó-nibúd' tyóploye, a tó vam búdyet khóladno.)
It is warm in the hotel.	В гости́нице тепло́. (V gastínitse tyepló.)
There is central heating in the hotel. (*Literally*: steam heating.)	В гости́нице парово́е отопле́ние. (V gastínitse paravóye ataplyéniye.)

THE VERB (contd.)

The forms of the Russian verb are: the infinitive, present, past, future (simple and compound), imperative and subjunctive. In addition, Russian verbs have categories of aspect and voice.

Characteristic Russian infinitive endings are: '-ть', e.g. 'бы́ть' (buít'), to be; 'спроси́ть' perf. (sprasít'), to ask; and '-ти', e.g. 'принести́' perf. (prinyestí), 'to bring'; 'идти́' imperf. (ittí), to go. Note, there is no 'to' before the Russian infinitive.

Some verbs end in '-ться' (-t'sya) or '-тись' (-tis'). These are so-called reflexive verbs, when action is directed at the speaker himself. Compare, for instance, the verbs 'мы́ть' imperf. (muít'), to wash (something or someone else), and 'мы́ться' imperf. (muít'sya) to wash (oneself).

THE VERB (contd.)

In conjugating the reflexive verbs the endings '-ся' and '-сь' are retained.

Some Russian reflexive verbs are translated into English as 'oneself,' 'myself,' 'himself,' e.g. 'одеваться' imperf. (adyevát'sya), to dress oneself.

Они хорошо одеваются. They dress (themselves) well. (Aní kharashó adyeváyutsya.)

Most Russian reflexive verbs, however, correspond to English verbs without reflexive pronouns, e.g. 'находиться' imperf. (nakhadít'sya), to be situated; 'возвратиться' perf. (vozvratít'sya), to come back, to return.

The 'Souvenirs' shop is on Kutuzov Avenue.	Магазин «Сувениры» находится на Кутузовском проспекте. (Magazín 'Suvyenírui' nakhóditsya na Kutúzofskom praspuéktye.)

On the tenses of the Russian verb see TENSES.
On the imperative see THE IMPERATIVE.

The Subjunctive

The subjunctive is always accompanied by 'бы' (bui). It expresses a wish or desire. Compare:

Я хотела поговорить с вами. (Ya khatyéla pagavarít' s vámi.)	I wanted to speak to you.
Я хотела бы поговорить с вами. (Ya khatyéla bui pagavarít' s vámi.)	I should like to speak to you.

Sometimes the subjunctive 'чтобы' (shtóbui)—in order that, whether—is used as the conjunction.

Я хочу́, что́бы вы прие́хали сюда́ ещё ра́з. (Ya khachú, shtóbui vui priyékhali syudá yeshchó ráz.)	I should like you to come here again.

The Imperative

Below are some of the more common verbs used in the *Imperative*. These forms of speech are employed in addressing several persons or in addressing one person politely (for which the plural is used in Russian).

Most Russian verbs form the Imperative by adding '-те' to the stem if it ends in a vowel, or '-ите' if the stem ends in a consonant.

Infinitive	Present Tense form	Root	Imperative
да́ть (dát') to give	даю́т (dayút) (they) give	да-	Да́йте! (Dáytye!) Give!
чита́ть (chitát') to read	чита́ет (chitáyet) (he) reads	чита́-	Чита́йте! (Chitáytye!) Read!
откры́ть (atkruít') to open	откро́ет (atkróyet) (he) will open	откро-	Откро́йте! (Atkróytye!) Open!
показа́ть (pakazát') to show	пока́жет (pakázhyet) (he) will show	покаж-	Покажи́те! (Pakazhítye!) Show!

THE IMPERATIVE

Infinitive	Present Tense form	Root	Imperative
принести́ (prinyestí) to bring	принесёт (prinyesyót) (he) will bring	принес-	Принеси́те! (Prinyesítye!) Bring!
подожда́ть (padazhdát') to wait	подождёт (padazhdyót) (he) will wait	подожд-	Подожди́те! (Padazhdítye!) Wait!

'Откры́ть', 'принести́', etc., are translated in the Future Tense because they are Perf. verbs (see the section on TENSES).

For the negative form of the Imperative see NEGATION.

In the Imperative, infinitives ending in '-ось' or '-ся' take '-есь', e.g., сади́тся (sadít'sya), to sit down: Сади́тесь! (Sadítyes'), Sit down! Take a seat!; расписа́ться (raspisát'sya), to sign (one's name): Распиши́тесь! (Raspishítyes'), Sign your name!

Here are some more sentences in the Imperative:

Give me some cigarettes, please.	Да́йте, пожа́луйста, сигаре́ты. (Dáytye, pazháluysta, sigaryétui.)
Take the medicine every day.	Принима́йте лека́рство ка́ждый де́нь. (Prinimáytye lyekárstvo kázhduiy dyén'.)
Show (me) these souvenirs.	Покажи́те э́ти сувени́ры. (Pakazhítye éti suvyenírui.)
Fill in this form.	Запо́лните э́тот бла́нк. (Zapólnitye étot blánk.)

Wake me at eight o'clock. Разбудите меня в восемь часов.
(Razbudítye myenyá v vósyem' chasóf.)

Go straight (on) and then to the left. Идите прямо и налево.
(Idítye pryámo i nalyévo.)

GENDER OF NOUNS

Russian nouns are either masculine, feminine or neuter. You can usually tell the gender of a noun by its ending.

Typical masculine endings are:

1. The consonants: '-п', '-м', '-н', '-р', '-с', '-т', '-д', '-к', '-з', '-ц', etc.:

август (ávgust), August; автобус (aftóbus), bus; архитектор (arkhityéktor), architect; номер (nómyer), number; переводчик (pyerevótchik), interpreter; ресторан (restarán), restaurant; банк (bánk), bank; билет (bilyét), ticket; город (górot), town; месяц (myésyats), month; сахар (sákhar), sugar; счёт (shchót), bill, or account; чемодан (chemadán), suitcase; экскурсовод (ekskursovót), guide.

2. A few masculine nouns end with the soft sign 'ь': апрель (apryél'), April; день (dyén'), day; дождь (dósht'), rain; рубль (rúbl'), rouble; словарь (slavár') dictionary.

3. And a few end with 'й':

май (máy), May; музей (muzyéi), museum; чай (chái), tea.

Typical feminine endings are:

1. 'а':

гостиница (gastínitsa), hotel; копейка (kapyéyka), copek; погода (pagóda), weather; посылка (pasuílka), parcel; почта (póchta), post, post-office; рыба (ruíba), fish;

GENDER OF NOUNS

сигаре́та (sigaryéta), cigarette; страна́ (straná), country.

2. '-я' and '-ия' ('ya' and 'iya'):

земля́ (zyemlyá), earth, land; консервато́рия (kansyervatóriya), conservatoire; ста́нция (stántsiya), station; тамо́жня (tamózhnya), Customs; фами́лия (famíliya), surname; экску́рсия (ekskúrsiya), excursion.

3. The soft sign 'ь':

ве́щь (vyéshch'), thing; о́сень (ósyen'), autumn; форма́льность (formál'nost'), formality; че́тверть (chétvyert'), quarter.

Neuter endings are '-о' or '-е' ('o' or 'ye' as in yes):
бюро́ (byuró), bureau, office; лека́рство (lyekárstvo), medicine; ле́то (lyéto), summer; молоко́ (malakó), milk; окно́ (aknó), window; пи́во (pívo), beer; письмо́ (pis'mó), letter; сло́во (slóvo), word; воскресе́нье (vaskryesyén'ye), Sunday; зда́ние (zdániye), building; кафе́ (kafé), café; обслу́живание (apslúzhivaniye), service; расписа́ние (raspisániye), timetable.

The gender of the noun determines the form of the *adjective* and *verb* (in the Past Tense) used with the noun, e.g.:

m. Formerly this town was small and ugly. Ра́ньше э́тот го́род был ма́ленький и некраси́вый.
(Rán'she étot górot buil mályen'kiy i nyekrasívui.)

f. Formerly this hotel was small and ugly. Ра́ньше э́та гости́ница была́ ма́ленькая и некраси́вая.
(Rán'she éta gastínitsa buíla mályen'kaya i nyekrasívaya.)

n. Formerly this building was small and ugly. Ра́ньше э́то зда́ние бы́ло ма́ленькое и некраси́вое. (Rán'she éto zdániye buílo mályen'koye i nyekrasívoye.)

Note how 'э́тот', 'ма́ленький', 'некраси́вый', 'был', change their form depending on the gender of the noun. For a more detailed explanation see ADJECTIVES, DEMONSTRATIVES and TENSES.

PLURAL OF NOUNS

It may seem at first sight that plural endings of nouns are quite numerous. However, it is not so in fact. There are only four plural noun endings, nowhere near as many as singular endings. They are:

The ending **'-ы'**: This ending helps to form the plural of nouns which in the singular end in any hard consonant or in '-а' (except when '-а' is preceded by '-к', '-г' or '-х').

'-и': This helps to form the plural of nouns which in the singular end in 'а' preceded by '-к', '-г' or '-х', or in '-к', '-г', '-х', or in any soft vowel and '-й'.

'-а': This is typical of nouns which in the singular end in '-о' and of a few nouns ending in a consonant.

'-я': this forms the plural of nouns ending in '-е' in the singular.

Now look through the examples below, which show the formation of the plural of some of the nouns appearing in this book.

The ending **'-ы'** of masculine nouns:

Singular	*Plural*
авто́бус (aftóbus), bus	авто́бусы (aftóbusui), buses
биле́т (bilyét), ticket	биле́ты (bilyétui), tickets

PLURAL OF NOUNS

зал (zal), hall	за́лы (zálui), halls
магази́н (magazín), shop	магази́ны (magazínui), shops
ме́сяц (mésyats), month	ме́сяцы (mésyatsui), months
рестора́н (restarán), restaurant	рестора́ны (restaránui), restaurants
собо́р (sabór), cathedral	собо́ры (sabórui), cathedrals
стака́н (stakán), glass	стака́ны (stakánui), glasses
стол (stol), table	столы́ (staluí), tables
сувени́р (suvyenír), souvenir	сувени́ры (suvyenírui), souvenirs
теа́тр (te-átr), theatre	теа́тры (te-átrui), theatres
телефо́н (tyelyefón), telephone	телефо́ны (tyelyefónui), telephones
тролле́йбус (tralléybus), trolleybus	тролле́йбусы (tralléybusui), trolleybuses
чемода́н (chemadán), suitcase	чемода́ны (chemadánui), suitcases
экскурсово́д (ekskursovót), guide	экскурсово́ды (ekskursovódui), guides

The ending '-ы' of feminine nouns:

голова́ (galavá), head	го́ловы (gólovui), heads
гости́ница (gastínitsa), hotel	гости́ницы (gastínitsui), hotels
жена́ (zhená), wife	жёны (zhónui), wives
ка́сса (kássa), cash desk	ка́ссы (kássui), cash desks
ко́мната (kómnata), room	ко́мнаты (kómnatui), rooms
мину́та (minúta), minute	мину́ты (minútui), minutes
сигаре́та (sigaryéta), cigarette	сигаре́ты (sigaryétui), cigarettes
страна́ (straná), country	стра́ны (stránui), countries

телегра́мма (tyelyegráma), telegram | телегра́ммы (tyelyegrámui), telegrams
у́лица (úlitsa), street | у́лицы (úlitsui), streets
цена́ (tsyená), price | це́ны (tsyénui), prices

Note that in forming the plural, the stress is often shifted.

The ending '-и' of masculine nouns:

ба́нк (bánk), bank | ба́нки (bánki), banks
бла́нк (blank), form | бла́нки (blánki), forms
до́ждь (dósht'), rain | дожди́ (dazhdí), rains
за́втрак (záftrak), breakfast | за́втраки (záftraki), breakfasts
клю́ч (klyúch), key | ключи́ (klyuchí), keys
музе́й (muzyéi), museum | музе́и (muzyéyi), museums
перево́дчик (pyeryevótchik), interpreter | перево́дчики (pyeryevótchiki), interpreters
ру́бль (rúbl'), rouble | рубли́ (rublí), roubles
слова́рь (slavár'), dictionary | словари́ (slavarí), dictionaries

The ending '-а' of neuter nouns:

де́ло (dyélo), business, things | дела́ (dyelá), things
лека́рство (lyekárstvo), medicine | лека́рства (lyekárstva), medicines
окно́ (aknó), window | о́кна (ókna), windows
письмо́ (pis'mó), letter | пи́сьма (pís'ma), letters
сло́во (slóvo), word | слова́ (slavá), words
число́ (chisló), number, date | чи́сла (chísla), numbers, dates

The ending '-а' of masculine nouns:

ве́к (vyék), century | века́ (vyeká), centuries

PLURAL OF NOUNS

го́род (górot), town	города́ (garadá), towns
но́мер (nómyer), number	номера́ (nomyerá), numbers
па́спорт (pásport), passport	паспорта́ (pasportá), passports
по́езд (póyest), train	поезда́ (payezdá), trains

N.B. *Exceptions to the rule*: Some nouns change in the plural, e.g.:

де́нь (dyén'), day	дни́ (dní), days
значо́к (znachók), badge	значки́ (znachkí), badges
пода́рок (padárok), gift	пода́рки (padárki), gifts

The ending '**-я**' of neuter nouns:

зда́ние (zdániye), building	зда́ния (zdániya), buildings
расписа́ние (raspisániye), timetable	расписа́ния (raspisániya), timetables

Nouns derived from adjectives form their plural in the same way as adjectives, by changing the last two vowels.

Singular	*Plural*
столо́вая (stalóvaya), dining-room	столо́вые (stalóvuiye), dining-rooms
парикма́херская (parikmákherskaya), barber's, hairdresser's	парикма́херские (parikmákherskiye), barbers', hairdressers'

The plural of a number of words borrowed into Russian from other languages coincides with the singular, e.g.:

Singular	*Plural*
бюро́ (byuró), bureau	бюро́, bureaux
кафе́ (kafé), café	кафе́, cafés
меню́ (myenyú), menu	меню́, menus
пальто́ (pal'tó), overcoat	пальто́, overcoats
такси́ (taksí), taxi	такси́, taxis

Some nouns have different stems in the singular and plural:

человéк (chelovyék), man — лю́ди (lyúdi), men
до́чь (dóch'), daughter — до́чери (dóchyeri), daughters
ма́ть (mát'), mother — ма́тери (mátyeri), mothers
ребёнок (rebyónok), child — дéти (dyéti), children

The nouns 'дéньги' (dyén'gi), money, and 'сýтки' (sútki), a 24-hour day-and-night period, and a few others, have no singular form.

ADJECTIVES

Russian adjectives agree with the nouns they qualify. They can be divided into 'hard,' 'soft,' and 'mixed.' The endings of the 'hard' adjectives are:

- **ый** (or **ой**, if the stress is on the last syllable), for the masculine singular
- **ая** for the feminine singular
- **ое** for the neuter singular
- **ые** for all genders in the plural.

The endings of the 'soft' adjectives are:

- **ий** for the masculine singular
- **яя** for the feminine singular
- **ее** for the neuter singular
- **ие** for all genders in the plural.

The endings of the 'mixed' adjectives:

- **ий** (or **ой**, if the stress is on the last syllable) for the masculine singular
- **ая** for the feminine singular
- **ое** for the neuter singular
- **ие** for all genders in the plural.

ADJECTIVES

m. но́вый го́род (nóvuiy górot), new town
f. но́вая у́лица (nóvaya úlitsa), new street
n. но́вое зда́ние (nóvoye zdániye), new building
pl. но́вые города́/у́лицы, зда́ния (nóvuiye garadá/úlitsui, zdániya), new towns, streets, buildings

More adjectives of this type:

краси́вый (krasívuiy), beautiful; дешёвый (dyeshóvuiy), cheap, inexpensive; дово́льный (davól'nuiy), content, pleased, satisfied; тру́дный (trúdnuiy), difficult; кра́сный (krásnuiy), red; си́льный (síl'nuiy), strong; уста́лый (ustáluiy), tired; поле́зный (palyéznuiy), useful; свобо́дный (svabódnuiy), free; здоро́вый (zdaróvuiy), healthy; голо́дный (galódnuiy), hungry; обы́чный (abuíchnuiy), usual; бе́лый (byéluiy), white.

большо́й магази́н (bal'shói magazín), m., large shop
больша́я гости́ница (bal'sháya gastínitsa), f., large hotel
большо́е зда́ние (bal'shóye zdániye), n., large building
больши́е магази́ны/гости́ницы/зда́ния (bal'shíye magazínui/gastínitsui/zdániya), pl., large shops/hotels/buildings

плохо́й (plakhói), bad; дорого́й (daragói), dear; больно́й (bal'nói), ill; друго́й (drugói), other; молодо́й (malodói), young.

ма́ленький рестора́н (málen'kiy restarán), m., small restaurant
ма́ленькая столо́вая (málen'kaya stalóvaya), f., small dining-room
ма́ленькое кафе́ (málen'koye kafé), n., small café
ма́ленькие рестора́ны, столо́вые, кафе́ (málen'kiye restaránui, kafé, stalóvuiye), pl., small restaurants, dining-rooms, cafés

московский (maskófskiy), belonging to or characteristic of Moscow; русский (rússkiy), Russian; советский (savyétskiy), Soviet.

Adjectives can either precede or follow the noun:
'хорошая погода' (kharóshaya pagóda) 'good weather'; or 'погода хорошая' (pagóda kharóshaya).
Погода была хорошая (Pagóda builá kharóshaya), The weather was fine.

Use of Short Forms

Don't say 'Он был довольный' (On buíl davól'nuiy) (He was satisfied), but say 'Он был доволен' (On buíl davólyen).

Note how the short forms are made:

m. довольный—доволен (davólyen), satisfied
f. довольная—довольна (davól'na)
n. довольное—довольно (davól'no)
pl. довольные—довольны (davól'nui)

m. больной—болен (bólyen), ill
f. больная—больна (bal'ná)
n. больное—больно (bal'nó)
pl. больные—больны (bal'nuí)

m. свободный—свободен (svabódyen), free
f. свободная—свободна (svabódna)
n. свободное—свободно (svabódno)
pl. свободные—свободны (svabódnui)

m. здоровый—здоров (zdaróf), healthy, well
f. здоровая—здорова (zdaróva)
n. здоровое—здорово (zdaróvo)
pl. здоровые—здоровы (zdaróvui)

ADJECTIVES

How do you feel?	Ка́к вы себя́ чу́вствуете?
(*Literally*: How do you yourself feel?)	(Kák vui syebyá chústvuyetye?)
Thank you, I am already quite well.	Спаси́бо, я уже́ совсе́м здоро́в.
	(Spasíbo, ya uzhé safsyém zdaróf.)
My wife is ill.	Моя́ жена́ больна́.
	(Mayá zhená bal'ná.)
Tell me, is this seat free?	Скажи́те, э́то ме́сто свобо́дно?
	(Skazhítye, éto myésto svabódno?)

As in English, Russian adjectives have three degrees of comparison: positive, comparative and superlative.

The simple form is the same for all three genders, e.g.

positive: m. тру́дный (trúdnuiy), difficult
 f. тру́дная (trúdnaya)
 n. тру́дное (trúdnoye)
 pl. тру́дные (trúdnuiye)
comparative: трудне́е (trudnyéye), more difficult

To my mind the Russian language is more difficult than the Italian.	По-мо́ему, ру́сский язы́к трудне́е, чем италья́нский.
	(Pa-móyemu, rússkiy yazuík trudnyéye chem ital'yánskiy.)

Some useful adjectives form their degree of comparison with a different word.

Positive	*Comparative*
хоро́ший, good	лу́чше, better
(kharóshiy)	(lútshe)

плохо́й, bad   ху́же, worse
(plakhói)   (khúzhe)
большо́й, large   бо́льше, larger
(bal'shói)   (ból'she)
ма́ленький, small   ме́ньше, smaller
(mályen'kiy)   (myén'she)
дорого́й, dear   доро́же, dearer
(daragói)   (darózhe)
молодо́й, young   моло́же, younger
(maladói)   (malózhe)

Complex comparisons are formed with 'бо́лее' (bólyeye), more, or 'ме́нее' (myényeye), less, used before the adjective:

совреме́нный (savryemyénnŭiy), modern

   бо́лее совреме́нный (bólyeye savryeménnuiy), more modern

   ме́нее совреме́нный (myényeye savryeménnuiy), less modern

This hotel is more modern than that (one).   Э́та гости́ница бо́лее совреме́нная, чем та́.
(Éta gastínitsa bólyeye savryemyénnaya, chem tá.)

We are staying in a more modern hotel.   Мы живём в бо́лее совреме́нной гости́нице.
(Mui zhivyóm v bólyeye savryemyénnoi gastínitse.)

They are also formed by the use of 'чём' (chém), than, or the Genitive of the noun or pronoun (the latter for the simple form only).

Leningrad is smaller than Moscow.   Ленингра́д ме́ньше Москвы́.
(Lyeningrát myén'she Maskvuí.)

ADJECTIVES

Leningrad is smaller than Moscow.	Ленингра́д ме́ньше, чем Москва́. (Lyeningrát myén'she, chem Maskvá.)
To my mind Leningrad is a more beautiful city than Moscow.	По-мо́ему, Ленингра́д бо́лее краси́вый го́род, чем Москва́. (Pa-móyemu, Lyeningrát bólyeye krasívuiy górot, chem Maskvá.)

The more frequent form of the superlative is 'са́мый, са́мая, са́мое, са́мые' (sámuiy, sámaya, sámoye, sámuiye), which precedes the adjective.

Positive	*Superlative*
m. большо́й, big, large	са́мый большо́й, biggest, largest
(bal'shói)	(sámuiy bal'shói)
f. больша́я	са́мая больша́я
(bal'sháya)	(sámaya bal'sháya)
n. большо́е	са́мое большо́е
(bal'shóye)	(sámoye bal'shóye)
pl. больши́е	са́мые больши́е
(bal'shíye)	(sámuiye bal'shíye)

The 'Rossia' Hotel is the largest hotel in Moscow.	Гости́ница «Росси́я»—са́мая больша́я гости́ница в Москве́. (Gastínitsa 'Rassíya'—sámaya bol'sháya gastínitsa v Maskvyé.)

Moscow is the largest city in the Soviet Union.	Москва—самый большой город в Советском Союзе.
	(Maskvá—sámuiy bal'shói górot v Savyétskom Sayúzye.)
The Moscow University building is the tallest in Moscow.	Здание Московского университета—самое высокое в Москве.
	(Zdániye Maskófskavo univyersityéta—sámoye vuisókoye v Maskvyé.)
In my opinion Russian forests are the most beautiful in the world.	По-моему, русские леса—самые красивые в мире.
	(Pa-móyemu, rússkiye lyesá—sámuiye krásivuiye v mírye.)
Today the weather is colder than yesterday.	Погода сегодня холоднее, чем вчера.
	(Pagóda syevódnya khaladnyéye, chem fcherá.)
He is younger than I.	Он моложе, чем я. или: Он моложе меня.
	(On malózhe chem yá) or (On malózhe myenyá.)
I think the trip to Suzdal is more interesting than the trip to Zagorsk.	Мне кажется, что поездка в Суздаль более интересная, чем поездка в Загорск.
	(Mnye kázhetsya, shto payéstka f Súzdal' bólyeye intyeryésnaya, chem payéstka v Zagórsk.)

DEMONSTRATIVES

The demonstrative pronouns 'этот' (étot), this, and 'тот' (tót), that, have three different gender forms in the singular and a common form in the plural.

m. этот сувенир, this souvenir (étot suvyenír)
 тот ресторан, that restaurant (tót restarán)

f. эта посылка, this parcel (éta pasuílka)
 та гостиница, that hotel (tá gastínitsa)

n. это окно, this window (éto aknó)
 то письмо, that letter (to pis'mó)

pl. эти сувениры, these souvenirs (éti souvyenírui)
 те рестораны, those restaurants (tye restaránui)

 эти посылки, these parcels (éti pasuílki)
 те гостиницы, those hotels (tye gastínitusi)

 эти окна, these windows (éti ókna)
 те письма, those letters (tye pís'ma)

'Тот' is used to indicate an object which is remote from the speaker, in contrast with one that is near.

Note that, unlike English practice, the demonstratives 'этот' and 'тот' can be used instead of nouns.

This table is occupied but that one is free.
 Этот стол занят, а тот свободен.
 (Étot stol zányat, a tót svabódyen.)

This hotel is more modern than that one.
 Эта гостиница более современная, чем та.
 Éta gastínitsa bólyeye sovryemyónnaya, chem tá.)

The neuter demonstrative adjective 'это' should not be confused with the pronoun 'это'. The latter means 'this is' or 'these are'.

When you learn the declension of nouns (see CASES OF NOUNS) and pronouns (see CASES OF PRONOUNS) remember that if you get the noun ending right, the adjective is not likely to cause misunderstanding.

The demonstrative adjectives have the following cases:

	Singular			Plural
	Masc.	*Fem.*	*Neuter*	*All genders*
Nom.	этот	эта	это	эти
	тот	та	то	те
Gen.	этого	этой	этого	этих
	того	той	того	тех
Acc.	этот	эту	это	эти (этих)
	этого	ту		те (тех)
	того			
Dat.	этому	этой	этому	этим
	тому	той	тому	тем
Instr.	этим	этой	этим	этими
	тем	той	тем	теми
Prep.	(об) этом	(об) этой	(об) этом	(об) этих
	(о) том	(о) той	(о) том	(о) тех

I want to look through these books. Я хочу посмотреть эти книги.
(Ya khachú pasmatryét' éti knígi.)

We are staying at this hotel. Мы живём в этой гостинице.
(Mui zhivyóm v étoi gastínitse.)

DEMONSTRATIVES

Tell us about this new district.	Расскажи́те нам об э́том но́вом райо́не. (Raskazhítye nam ob étom nóvom rayónye.)
This is Gorky Street.	Э́то у́лица Го́рького. (Éto úlitsa Gór'kavo.)
This is the new stadium.	Э́то но́вый стадио́н. (Éto nóvuiy stadión.)
These are Russian souvenirs.	Э́то ру́сские сувени́ры. (Éto rússkiye suvyenírui.)

ADVERBS

Adverbs are usually added to verbs and occasionally to adjectives or other adverbs—much the same as in English.

Мне о́чень нра́вится моро́женое. (Mnye óchen' nrávitsya marózhenoye.)	I like icecream very much.
Здесь о́чень хоро́шие сувени́ры. (Zdyes' óchen' kharóshiye suvyenírui.)	There are very good souvenirs here.
Вы о́чень хорошо́ говори́те по англи́йски. (Vui óchen' kharashó gavarítye pa-anglíyski.)	You speak English very well.

They can be placed either before or after a verb.

Here are some useful adverbs:

сейча́с (seichás), now; давно́ (davnó), long ago; неда́вно (nyedávno), recently; сего́дня (syevódnya), today; вчера́ (fcherá), yesterday; всегда́ (fsyegdá) always; иногда́ (inagdá), sometimes; никогда́ (nikagdá), never; ре́дко (ryétko), seldom; ча́сто (chásto), frequently; за́втра (záftra), tomorrow; у́тром (útrom), in the morning; ве́чером (vyécherom), in the evening; зимо́й (zimói), in winter; ле́том (lyétom), in summer; ско́ро (skóro), soon; снача́ла (snachála), firstly; пото́м (patóm), later on, then; опя́ть (apyát'), again; тогда́ (tagdá), then.

Adverbs of place and motion:
здесь (zdyés'), here; сюда́ (syudá), here; там (tám), there; туда́ (tudá), there; где (gdyé), where; куда́ (kudá), where; до́ма (dóma), at home; домо́й (damói), home; заграни́цей (zagranítsey) abroad; заграни́цу (zagranítsu) abroad.

Unlike English, Russian has different adverbs to show both the place and the direction of an action. Adverbs of place are used with 'static' verbs ('быть', 'находи́ться', to be, to be situated), while adverbs of motion are used with verbs of motion ('идти́', 'е́хать', to go, to walk). The following examples demonstrate this:

Where is the 'Druzhba' shop?	Где нахо́дится магази́н «Дру́жба»?
	(Gdyé nakhóditsya magazín 'Drúzhba'?)
Where are you going in the evening?	Куда́ вы пойдёте ве́чером?
	(Kudá vui paydyótye vyécherom?)
Have you been to Vladimir?	Вы бы́ли во Влади́мире?
	(Vui buíli vo Vladímirye?)
Yes, I have already been there. I have not been to Leningrad. When can I go there?	Да, я там уже́ был. Я не́ был в Ленингра́де. Когда́ мо́жна туда́ пое́хать?
	(Da, ya tam uzhé buíl. Ya nyé

ADVERBS

buil v Lyeningrádye. Kogdá
mózhna tudá payékhat'?)

Many adverbs are derived from adjectives by changing the ending to '-o'.

Adjectives	*Adverbs*
хоро́ший (kharóshiy), good	хорошо́ (kharashó), well
плохо́й (plakhói), bad	пло́хо (plókho), badly
свобо́дный (svabódnuiy), free	свобо́дно (svabódno), freely

Compare:

The weather is fine today.	Пого́да сего́дня хоро́шая. (Adj.)
	(Pagóda syevódnya kharóshaya.)
I feel fine.	Я чу́вствую себя́ хорошо́. (Adv.)
	(Ya chústvuyu syebyá kharashó.)
Tell me, is this seat free?	Скажи́те, э́то ме́сто свобо́дно? (Adj.)
	(Skazhítye, éto myésto svabódno?)
My wife speaks French fluently.	Моя́ жена́ свобо́дно говори́т по-францу́зски. (Adv.)
	(Mayá zhená svabódno gavarít pa-frantsúski.)

The last-mentioned example shows that an adverb ending in '-o' coincides with the *short form* of the *adjective* of the neuter gender. In addition, the form ending in '-o' can be the *predicate* of an *impersonal* sentence.

It is fine here.	Здесь о́чень хорошо́.
	(Zdyes' óchen' kharashó.)
It is cold today.	Сего́дня хо́лодно.
	(Syevódnya khólodno.)
I am cold.	Мне́ хо́лодно.
(*Literally*: to me it is cold.)	(Mnyé khólodno.)
Are you unwell? (Are you feeling unwell?)	Вам пло́хо? (Вы пло́хо себя́ чу́вствуете?)
	(Vam plókho? (Vui plókho sebyá chústvuyetye?))

Adverbs form the comparative in the same way as adjectives. They form the superlative by adding 'всего́' (fsyevó) after the comparative.

Positive	*Comparative*	*Superlative*
хо́лодно, cold	холодне́е, colder	холодне́е всего́, coldest of all
(khólodno)	(khaladnyéye)	(khaladnyéye fsyevó)
хорошо́, good	лу́чше, better	лу́чше всего́, best of all
(kharashó)	(lútshe)	(lútshe fsyevó)

Age

How old are you?	Ско́лько ва́м ле́т?
(*Literally*: How many years to you?)	(Skól'ko vám lyét?)
I am twenty years old.	Мне́ два́дцать ле́т.
	(Mnyé dváttsat' lyét.)

If you address this question to a child, you use the 'intimate' form of speaking (see note regarding the use of the 2nd person singular, on p. 23).

How old are you?	Ско́лько тебе́ ле́т?
	(Skól'ko tyebyé lyét?)
I am twelve years old.	Мне́ двена́дцать ле́т.
	(Mnyé dvyenáttsat' lyet.)

The difference between 'вам' and 'тебе́' is the same as between 'вы' (vui), which is used with grown-ups and strangers, and 'ты' (tui) which, as already explained, is used with children, relatives and close friends.

Today is my birthday.	Сего́дня у меня́ де́нь рожде́ния.
	(Syevódnya u myenyá dyén' razhdyéniya.)
Many happy returns of the day!	Поздравля́ю с днём рожде́ния!
(*Literally*: I congratulate you for your birthday!)	(Pazdravlyáyu s dnyóm razhdyéniya!)

To Agree

I agree with you.	Я с ва́ми согла́сен.
	(Ya s vami saglásyen.)
My wife does not agree.	Моя́ жена́ не согла́сна.
	(Mayá zhená nyé saglásna.)
Do you agree to go to Kiev tomorrow?	Вы согла́сны пое́хать в Ки́ев за́втра?
	(Vui saglásnui payékhat' v Kíyef záftra?)

The short-form adjective 'согла́сен (согла́сна, согла́сны)' plays the role of a predicate, agreeing with the subject in gender and number.

In the Past Tense, however, the verbs 'соглаша́ться'

(saglashát'sya) imperf. and 'согласи́ться' (saglasít'sya) perf. are more common.

For a long time he would not agree to come.	Он до́лго не соглаша́лся прие́хать.
	(On dólgo nye saglashálsya priyékhat'.)
She agreed to come at once.	Она́ сра́зу согласи́лась прие́хать.
	(Oná srázu saglasílas' priyékhat'.)

To express the Future Tense 'согласи́ться' is generally used, e.g.:

I think they will agree to do it.   Я ду́маю, они́ соглася́тся сде́лать э́то.

(Ya dúmayu, aní saglasyátsya sdyélat' éto.)

PRONOUNS

Russian personal pronouns generally have the same functions as English pronouns.

я (ya)	I	мы (mui)	we
ты (tui)	you (thou)	вы (vui)	you
он (on)	he	они́ (aní)	they
она́ (oná)	she		

'Вы' can refer to one or several persons, like the English 'you'. It is the polite and formal way of addressing one person. The familiar form (used in speaking to an intimate friend, a close relative, or a child) is 'ты'.

Kolya, do you want to go to the cinema?   Ко́ля, ты хо́чешь пойти́ в кино́?

(Kólya, tui khóchesh' paytí f kinó?)

PRONOUNS

Nikolai Ivanovich, would you like to go on an excursion?	Николай Иванович, вы хотите поехать на экскурсию? (Nikalái Ivánovich, vui khatítye payékhat' na eksúrsiyu?)

'Он' can be used instead of a masculine noun, whether denoting a person or thing. 'Она' is a substitute for any feminine noun. Therefore 'он' corresponds to 'he' and 'it', and 'она' to 'she' and 'it'.

I want to buy a samovar. How much does it cost?	Я хочу купить самовар. Сколько он стоит? (Ya khachú kupít' samovár. Skól'ko on stó-it?)
We want to go to the exhibition. Where is it?	Мы хотим поехать на выставку. Где он находится? (Mui khatím payékhat' na vuístafku. Gdyé oná nakhóditsya?)

Cases of Pronouns

Some case forms of personal pronouns are very often used and should be learned.

	I	*WE*	*YOU*
Nom.	я (ya)	мы (mui)	вы (vui)
Gen.	меня (myenyá)	нас (nas)	вам (vas)
Dat.	мне (mnyé)	нам (nam)	вам (vam)
Acc.	меня (myenýa)	нас (nas)	вас (vas)

	HE		*SHE*		*THEY*	
Nom.	он	(on)	она́	(oná)	они́	(aní)
Gen.	его́	(yevó)	её	(yeyó)	их	(ikh)
Dat.	ему́	(yemú)	ей	(yey)	им	(im)
Acc.	его́	(yevó)	её	(yeyó)	их	(ikh)

The genitive with the preposition 'y' expresses possession.

I have some cigarettes. У меня́ е́сть сигаре́ты.
(U myenyá yést' sigaryétui.)

They have tickets. У них е́сть биле́ты.
(U nikh yést' bilyétui.)

Following this preposition 'его́', 'её' and 'их' become '(у) него́', '(у) неё', '(у) них'. (Note: 'г' pronounced 'v'.)

The dative is used.

1. In sentences with the verb 'нра́виться' (nrávit'sya), to like; 'каза́ться' (kazát'sya), to seem, and some others.

Do you like this hotel? Вам нра́вится э́та гости́ница?
(Vam nrávitsya éta gastínitsa?)

We don't like this room. Нам не нра́вится э́та ко́мната.
(Nam nye nrávitsya éta kómnata.)

I believe (it seems to me) that I have a temperature. Мне ка́жется, что у меня́ температу́ра.
(Mnye kázhetsya, shto u menyá tempyeratúra.)

2. In discussing a person's physical feeling:

Are you cold? Вам хо́лодно?
(Vam khólodno?)

I am hot. Мне жа́рко.
(Mnyé zhárko.)

3. In discussing age.
How old are you? Ско́лько вам лет?
(*Literally*: How many years (Skól'ko vam lyét?)
  to you?)
I am thirty-five years old. Мне три́дцать пять лет.
(*Literally*: To me are . . .) (Mnyé tríttsat' pyat' lyét.)
The Accusative is used in the following sentences:
What is your name? Как вас зову́т?
(Kák vás zavút?)
My name is Peter Johnson. Меня́ зову́т Пи́тер Джо́нсон.
(Myenyá zavút Pítyer Dzhónson.)

INTERROGATIVES

The commonest interrogative words are:
кто (kto), who где (gdye), where
что (shto), what куда́ (kudá), where
чей (chei), whose отку́да (atkúda), from where
како́й (kakói), what, which как (kak), how
почему́ (pochemú), why ско́лько (skól'ko), how
зачем (zachém), why   many, how much

Grammatically speaking, 'кто' is a masculine singular. So the verb must *always* be singular and have a *masculine ending* (in the Past Tense) even if the question concerns several persons or one of the female sex.

Who wanted to go on a Кто хоте́л пое́хать на экс-
  tour round Moscow?   ку́рсию по Москве́?
(Któ khatyél payékhat' na ekskúrsiyu pa Maskvyé?)

'Чей' and 'какой' precede the noun and agree with it in gender and number, e.g.

What day (of the week) is it today?	Какой сегодня день? (Kakói syevódnya dyén'?)
What date is it today?	Какое сегодня число? (Kakóye syevódnya chisló?)
What records do you want to buy?	Какие пластинки вы хотите купить? (Kakíye plastínki vui khatítye kupít'?)

In interrogative sentences 'чей' often goes together with 'это', e.g.:

Whose suitcase is this?	Чей это чемодан? (m.) (Chéi éto chemodán?)
Whose bag is this?	Чья это сумка? (f.) (Ch'yá éta súmka?)
Whose letter is this?	Чьё это письмо? (n.) (Ch'yó éto pis'mó?)
Whose things are these?	Чьи это вещи? (pl.) (Ch'í éto vyéshchi?)

To discriminate between 'где' and 'куда' see ADVERBS.

'Сколько' is used both with countable and abstract nouns.

How many stamps do you want to buy?	Сколько марок вы хотите купить? (Skól'ko márok vui khatítye kupít'?)
How much milk shall we take?	Сколько молоко мы возьмём? (Skól'ko malakó mui vaz'myóm?)

The difference is that countable nouns are put in the Genitive plural and abstract nouns in the Genitive singular.

To Invite

Imperf. Приглаша́ть (priglashát')
Present:
I invite	я приглаша́ю	(ya priglasháyu)
you invite	вы приглаша́ете	(vui priglasháyetye)
they invite	они́ приглаша́ют	(aní priglasháyut)

Perf. Пригласи́ть (priglasít')
Future:
I will invite	я приглашу́	(ya priglashú)
we will invite	мы пригласи́м	(mui priglasím)
they will invite	они́ пригласи́т	(aní priglasyát)

Past:
I/he invited	я/он пригласи́л (m.)	(ya/on priglasíl)
I/she invited	я/она́ пригласи́ла (f.)	(ya/oná priglasíla)
we/they invited	мы/они́ пригласи́ли (pl.)	(mui/aní priglasíli)

Imperative: Invite! Пригласи́те! (Priglasítye!)

We invite you to our place.	Мы приглаша́ем ва́с в го́сти. (Mui priglasháyem vás v gosti.)
I shall invite my friends to an evening (party).	Я приглашу́ свои́х друзе́й на ве́чер. (Ya priglashú svaíkh druzyéy na vyécher.)
He invited me to the theatre.	Он пригласи́л меня́ в теа́тр. (On priglasíl myenyá f te-átr.)

SPEAK, READ, WRITE RUSSIAN

To Know

Imperf. Знать (znat')
Present:
I know	я зна́ю	(ya znáyu)
you know	вы зна́ете	(vui znáyetye)
he knows	он зна́ет	(on znáyet)
we know	мы зна́ем	(mui znáyem)
they know	они́ зна́ют	(aní znáyut)

Future:
I shall know	я бу́ду знать	(ya búdu znat')
you will know	вы бу́дете знать	(vui búdyetye znat')
he will know	он бу́дет знать	(on búdyet znat')
we shall know	мы бу́дем знать	(mui búdyem znat')
they will know	они́ бу́дут знать	(aní búdut znat')

I know that the plane leaves in the morning.	Я зна́ю, что́ самолёт улета́ет у́тром.
	(Ya znáyu, shto samalyót ulyetáyet útrom.)
Do you know at what time the plane leaves?	Вы зна́ете, в кото́ром часу́ улета́ет самолёт?
	(Vui znáyetye, v katórom chasú ulyetáyet samolyót?)
We did not know that you had already arrived.	Мы не зна́ли, что вы уже́ прие́хали.
	(Mui nye ználi, shto vui uzhé priyékhali.)
Now I shall know where to buy good souvenirs.	Тепе́рь я бу́ду зна́ть, где мо́жно купи́ть хоро́шие сувени́ры.
(*Literally*: Now I shall know where it is possible to buy ...)	(Tyepyér' ya búdu znát', gdyé mózhno kupít' kharóshiye suvyenírui.)

118

TO ALLOW (LET)

To Allow (Let)

'Пу́сть' (púst') is used to express requests or advice involving a third person, e.g.:

Let him ring me tomorrow.	Пу́сть он позво́нит мне́ за́втра.
	(Púst' on pazvónit mnyé záftra.)
Let them see some new magazines.	Пу́сть они́ посмо́трят но́вые журна́лы.
	(Púst' aní pasmótryat nóvuiye zhurnálui.)

When making a request or recommendation directly to the person or persons concerned, 'дава́йте' (daváytye) is used:

Let us have a rest!	Дава́йте отдохнём!
	(Daváytye atdakhnyóm!)
Let us have a cup of coffee!	Дава́йте вы́пьем ча́шку ко́фе!
(*Literally*: . . . drink a cup . . .)	(Daváytye vuíp'yem cháshku kófe!)
Let us go to the exhibition!	Дава́йте пое́дем на вы́ставку!
	(Daváytye payédyem na vuístafku!)

When asking permission to do something, 'разреши́те' (razreshítye) is used:

Let (allow) me (to) see.	Разреши́те мне́ посмотре́ть.
	(Razreshítye mnyé pasmatryét'.)
Let (me) pass (allow me to pass).	Разреши́те пройти́.
	(Razreshítye praytí.)

SPEAK, READ, WRITE RUSSIAN

To Live, To Stay

Imperf. **Жить** (zhit')

Present:
I live	я живу́	(ya zhivú)
you live	вы живёте	(vui zhivyótye)
he lives	он живёт	(on zhivyót)
we live	мы живём	(mui zhivyóm)
they live	они́ живу́т	(aní zhivút)

Past:
I/he lived	я/он жил	(ya/on zhil) (m.)
I/she lived	я/она́ жила́	(ya/oná zhilá) (f.)
we/they lived	мы/они́ жи́ли	(mui/aní zhíli) (pl.)

Future:
I shall live	я бу́ду жить	(ya búdu zhit')
you will live	вы бу́дете жить	(vui búdyetye zhit')
he will live	он бу́дет жить	(on búdyet zhit')
we shall live	мы бу́дем жить	(mui búdyem zhit')
they will live	они́ бу́дут жить	(aní búdut zhit')

Where do you live now? — Где́ вы сейча́с живёте?
(Gdyé vui seichás zhivyótye?)

We are staying at the 'Ukraina' hotel. — Мы живём в гости́нице «Украи́на».
(Mui zhivyóm v gastínitsye 'Ukraína'.)

Where did you stay in Leningrad? — Где́ вы жи́ли в Ленингра́де?
(Gdyé vui zhíli v Lyeningrádye?)

You will live in the centre of town. — Вы бу́дете жи́ть в це́нтре го́рода.
(Vui búdyetye zhít' v tséntrye górodа.)

Liquid Refreshments

I am thirsty.	Я хочу́ пить.
(*Literally*: I want to drink.)	(Ya khachú pit'.)
Here is a café.	Вот кафе́.
	(Vót kafé.)
Let's go into that café.	Дава́йте зайдём в э́то кафе́.
	(Daváytye zaydyóm v éto kafé.)
Here we can have tea, coffee, fruit juices, mineral water ...	Здесь есть чай, ко́фе, фрукто́вые со́ки, минера́льная вода́ ...
(*Literally*: Here is etc.)	(Zydés' yést' chái, kófye, fruktóvuiye sóki, minerál'naya vadá ...)
What shall we (have to) drink?	Что мы бу́дем пить?
	(Shtó mui búdyem pít'?)
Shall we have tea or coffee?	Возьмём чай и́ли ко́фе?
(*Literally*: Shall we take, etc.)	(Vaz'myóm chái íli kófye?)
I always have white coffee.	Я всегда́ пью ко́фе с молоко́м.
(*Literally*: ... drink coffee with milk.)	(Ya fsyegdá p'yu kófye s malakóm.)
But I prefer black coffee.	А я предпочита́ю чёрный ко́фе.
	(A yá pryetpachitáyu chórnuiy kófye.)
Do you want (some) sugar?	Хоти́те са́хару?
	(Khatítye sákharu?)

Note that 'to have' is translated here as 'пить' (pit'), drink: 'пить ко́фе', to drink coffee.

SPEAK, READ, WRITE RUSSIAN

I should like to have a glass of tea.	Я вы́пил бы стака́н ча́я. (Ya vuípil bui stakán cháya.)

(*Literally*: I would drink, etc.)

'Бы' is used as 'should', 'would'.

a bottle of beer	буты́лку пи́ва (butuílku píva)
some wine	немно́го вина́ (nyemnógo viná)
some cognac	немно́го коньяка́ (nyemnógo kon'yaká)
some vodka	немно́го во́дки (nyemnógo vótki)
some champagne	немно́го шампа́нского (nyemnógo shampánskovo)

When mentioning a definite quantity of drink the Genitive is used with the name of the drink (see CASES OF NOUNS).

Let's have a drink.	Дава́йте вы́пьем. (Daváytye vuíp'yem.)
Give us, please, a hundred grammes of cognac, (some) coffee and ice-cream.	Да́йте нам, пожа́луйста, сто грамм коньяка́, ко́фе и моро́женое. (Dáytye nam, pazháluysta, sto gramm kan'yaká, kófye i marozhénoye.)
Your health! (*Literally*: for or to ...)	За ва́ше здоро́вье! (Za váshe zdaróv'ye!)
To friendship!	За дру́жбу! (Za drúzhbu!)
Something more?	Что́-нибу́дь ещё? (Shtó-nibúd' yeshchó?)

122

LIQUID REFRESHMENTS

No, thank you.	Нét, спасибо. (Nyét, spasíbo.)
Let me have the bill, please.	Дáйте, пожáлуйста, счёт. (Dáytye, pazháluysta, shchót.)
One rouble fifty copeks.	Один рубль пятьдесят копéек. (Adín rúbl' pyatdyesyát kapéyek.)
I have ten roubles.	У меня дéсять рублéй. (U myenyá dyésyat' rublyéi.)
Here is your change. Eight roubles fifty copeks. (*Literally*: Take the change, etc.)	Возьмите сдáчу. Восемь рублéй пятьдесят копéек. (Vaz'mítye sdáchu. Vósyem' rublyéi pyatdesyát kapéyek.)

To Like, To Love, To Prefer, etc.

Imperf. Любить (lyubít')
Present:

I like/love	я люблю	(ya lyublyú)
you like/love	вы любите	(vui lyúbitye)
he likes/loves	он любит	(on lyúbit)
we like/love	мы любим	(mui lyúbim)
they like/love	они любят	(aní lyúbyat)

Imperf.: Нрáвиться (nrávit'sya)
Present:

I like this thing	Мне нрáвится эта вéщь.	(sing.)
	(Mnyé nrávitsya éta vyéshch'.)	
I like these things	Мне нрáвятся эти вéщи.	(pl.)
	(Mnyé nrávyatsya éti vyéshchi.)	

you like	вам нра́вится	(sing.)
	(vam nrávitsya)	
	вам нра́вятся	(pl.)
	(vam nrávyatsya)	

This verb uses the personal pronoun in the Dative (see CASES OF PRONOUNS).

Perf. Понравиться (panrávit'sya)

Past:

I liked	мне́ понра́вился	m. sing.
	(mnyé panrávilsya)	
	мне́ понра́вилась	f. sing.
	(mnyé panrávilas')	
	мне́ понра́вились	plural
	(mnyé panrávilis')	

Future:

I shall like	мне́ понра́вится	sing.
	(mnyé panrávitsya)	
	мне́ понра́вятся	pl.
	(mnyé panrávyatsya)	

The verb 'люби́ть', 'to love', expresses a stronger emotion. It usually indicates the speaker's familiarity with the thing referred to. Compare the following:

Yesterday I was in the Pushkin Museum for the first time. I liked this museum very much.	Вчера́ я в пе́рвый ра́з был в музе́е Пу́шкина. Э́тот музе́й мне́ о́чень понра́вился.
	(Fcherá ya f pyérvuiy ráz buil v muzyéye Púshkina. Étot muzyéi mnyé óchen' panrávilsya.)

TO LIKE, TO LOVE, TO PREFER, ETC.

We often go to the Pushkin Museum. We are very fond of this museum.	Мы часто ходим в музей Пушкина. Мы очень любим этот музей. (Mui chásto khódim v muzyéi Púshkina. Mui óchen' lyúbim étot muzyéi.)
I am very fond of music.	Я очень люблю музыку. (Ya óchen' lyublyú múzuiku.)
Did you like the film 'War and Peace'?	Вам понравился фильм «Война и мир»? (Vam panrávilsya fíl'm 'Voiná i mír'?)
Are you fond of opera?	Вы любите оперу? (Vui lyúbitye óperu?)
I prefer ballet.	Я предпочитаю балет. (Yá pryetpachitáyu balyét.)
I like your proposal.	Мне нравится ваше предложение. (Mnyé nrávitsya váshe pryedlozhéniye.)
I know this town well and love it.	Я хорошо знаю и люблю этот город. (Ya kharashó znáyu i lyublyú étot górot.)
I like Russian folk songs.	Мне нравятся русские народные песни. (Mnyé nrávyatsya rússkiye naródnuiye pyésni.)

125

To Make, To Do

Imperf. Делать (dyélat')
Present:
I make/do	я делаю	(ya dyélayu)
you make/do	вы делаете	(vui dyélayetye)
they make/do	они делают	(aní dyélayut)

Perf. Сделать (zdyélat')
Future:
I will make	я сделаю	(ya zdyélayu)
you will make	вы сделаете	(vui zdyélayetye)
they will make	они сделают	(aní zdyélayut)

Past:
I made/did	я/он сделал m.	(ya/on zdyélal)
	я/она сделала f.	(ya/oná zdyélala)
we/they made/did	мы/они сделали pl.	(mui/aní zdyélali)

Imperative:
Make! Do!	Сделайте!	(Zdyélaytye!)
Don't make/do!	Не делайте!	(Nye dyélaytye!)

What are you doing now? Что вы сейчас делаете?
(Shtó vui seichás dyélayetye?)

He did everything he could. Он сделал всё, что мог.
(On zdyélal fsyó, shto móg.)

I can't do that. Я не могу этого сделать.
(Ya nye magú étovo zdyélat'.)

Please, do it today. Сделайте это сегодня, пожалуйста.
(Zdyélaytye éto syevódnya, pazháluysta.)

I'll do it tomorrow without fail. Я обязательно сделаю это завтра.
(Ya abyazátyel'no zdyélayu éto záftra.)

TO MAKE, TO DO

She made a mistake.	Она́ сде́лала оши́бку.
	(Oná zdyélala ashípku.)
The train does 70 km. an hour.	По́езд де́лает се́мьдесят киломе́тров в ча́с.
	(Póyest dyélayet syém'dyesyat kilomyétrof f chás.)
What are you doing tonight?	Что́ вы де́лаете сего́дня ве́чером?
	(Shtó vui dyélayetye syevódnya vyécherom?)

CASES OF NOUNS

Relationships of words in a sentence are expressed in English with the help of word order or prepositions. Take these three sentences:

John loves Mary.
Mary loves John.
I am writing a letter to my friend John.

John is the *subject* of the first sentence, the *direct object* in the *second sentence*, and *part* of the *indirect object* (indicating the addressee of the action) in the *third sentence*.

In Russian the *direct* and *indirect objects* and the *subject* all have different endings. Compare:

Джо́н лю́бит Ме́ри. (Dzhón lyúbit Meri.)
Ме́ри лю́бит Джо́на. (Méri lyúbit Dzhóna.)
Я пишу́ письмо́ своему́ дру́гу Джо́ну. (Ya pishú pis'mó svayemú drúgu Dzhónu.)

The different endings show the nouns in different cases.

Russian has six cases: the *Nominative, Genitive, Accusative, Dative, Instrumental* and *Prepositional*. Each noun has different case endings, depending on its gender and root.

Let us spend a little time now on the declension of nouns.

The *Nominative Case* is used to denote the subject of a sentence.

Suzdal is an ancient Russian city. Су́здаль—стари́нный ру́сский го́род.
(Súzdal'—starínnuiy rússkiy górot.)

The *Genitive Case*. Typical endings:

1. *Masculine* nouns ending in a hard consonant take **'-a'** (-a) in the singular and **'-ов'** (-of) in the plural.

Nominative Sing.: автобус, билет, город—bus, ticket, town (aftóbus, bilyét, górot)

Genitive sing.: автобуса, билета, города

Genitive pl.: автобусов, билетов, городов

2. *Feminine* nouns singular change **'-a'** (-a) to **'-ы'** (-ui) or to **'-и'** (-i) if the last consonant is 'г' or 'к':

Nominative Sing.: гости́ница, ко́мната, кни́га, ма́рка— hotel, room, book, stamp (gastínitsa, kómnata, kníga, márka)

Genitive sing.: гости́ницы, ко́мнаты, кни́ги, ма́рки

Genitive pl.: гости́ниц, ко́мнат, книг, ма́рок

3. *Neuter* nouns change **'-o'** (-o) to **'-a'** (-a) and **'-e'** (-ye) to **'-я'** (-ya).

The plural is mostly formed in the same way as for feminine nouns.

Nominative sing.: сло́во, окно́, зда́ние, word, window, building (slóvo, aknó, zdániye)

Genitive sing.: сло́ва, окна́, зда́ния

Genitive pl.: слов, о́кон, зда́ний

The *Genitive case* is used:

1. To express possession (see POSSESSION).
2. To describe the relation between two objects:

CASES OF NOUNS

но́мер телефо́на (nómyer tyelyefóna), telephone number—
No. of the telephone.

окна́ ко́мнаты (okná kómnatui), windows *of the* room.

3. When quantity is mentioned: стака́н молока́ (stakán malaká), glass of milk; ча́шка ча́я (cháshka cháya), cup of tea.

You will have noticed that these examples of the Genitive correspond to the English 'of'.

4. After words denoting quantity: 'мно́го' (mnógo), much, many; 'ма́ло' (málo), few, little; 'не́сколько' (nyéskol'ko), some, a few; 'ско́лько' (skól'ko), how many, how much; мно́го молока́ (mnógo malaká), much milk; ма́ло са́хара (málo sákhara), little sugar; мно́го городо́в (mnógo garadóf), many towns; не́сколько гости́ниц (nyéskol'ko gastínits), several hotels; ско́лько слов (skól'ko slof), how many words.

5. After numerals: after 2, 3 and 4—*Genitive singular*; after 5, 6, 7 etc.—*Genitive plural*: два биле́та (dva bilyéta), two tickets; два окна́ (dva akná), two windows; две гости́ницы (dvye gastínitsui), two hotels; пять биле́тов (pyat' bilyétof), five tickets; пять о́кон (pyat' ókon), five windows; пять гости́ниц (pyat' gastínits), five hotels.

6. To express a direct object governed by a negative verb. (See NEGATION.)

The *Dative Case* of nouns is not considered here, as it is used relatively seldom. For the *Dative of pronouns* see CASES OF PRONOUNS.

The *Accusative Case*. Typical endings:

1. The *Accusative* of *masculine nouns* denoting *inanimate* objects, and of all neuter nouns, has the same form as the *Nominative*.

E

This is a good wine.	Это хорошее вино.
	(n., Nomin.)
	(Éto kharósheye vinó.)
Give me this wine.	Дайте мне это вино.
	(n., Accus.)
	(Dáytye mnyé éto vinó.)
This is a new district.	Это новый район.
	(m., Nomin.)
	(Éto nóvuiy rayón.)
I should like to see this district.	Я хочу посмотреть этот район. (m., Accus.)
	(Ya khachú pasmatryét' étot rayón.)

2. The *Accusative* of *masculine nouns* denoting people and animals has the same form as the Genitive both in the *singular* and *plural*.

We are waiting for the interpreter.	Мы ждём переводчика.
	(Accus.)
	(Mui zhdyóm pyeryevótchika.)
This is the interpreter's dictionary.	Это словарь переводчика.
	(Genit.)
	(Éto slavár' pyeryevótchika.)

3. *Feminine nouns* ending in '**-a**' (-a) change 'a' for '**-y**' (-u).

Show (me) this book.	Покажите эту книгу.
Let (me) see this book.	(Accus.)
	(Pakazhítye étu knígu.)
I should like to buy a nest of dolls.	Я хотел бы купить матрёшку. (Accus.)
	(Ya khatyél bui kupít' matryóshku.)

CASES OF NOUNS

4. In the plural the *Accusative* is the same as the *Nominative* in all cases except those mentioned in (2).

Here are the tickets.	Вот билéты. (Vót bilyétui.)
Give me the tickets. (Let me have the tickets.)	Дáйте билéты. (Dáytye bilyétui.)
Here are some records.	Вот пластинки. (Vót plastínki.)
I bought some records.	Я купи́л пластинки. (Ya kupíl plastínki.)

The *Accusative* is used to express the *direct object* governed by transitive verbs like 'читáть', to read; 'писáть', to write; 'дáть', to give; 'купи́ть', to buy; 'показáть', to show, etc.

On the use of the *Accusative* with *prepositions* see IN/INTO and PREPOSITIONS.

The *Instrumental Case*. Typical endings:

1. *Masculine* and *neuter* nouns singular end in **'-ом'** or in **'-ем'** (-om) or (-yem).

Nominative: архитéктор (arkhityéktor) architect
переводчик (pyeryevótchik) interpreter
экскурсовод (ekskursavód) guide
молоко (malakó) milk
Instrumental: архитéктором (arkhityéktorom)
переводчиком (pyeryevótchikom)
экскурсоводом (ekskursavódom)
молоком (malakóm)

2. *Feminine* nouns change their Nominative ending **'-a'** (-a) to **'-ой'** or **'-ей'** (-oi or -yey).

Nominative: комната (kómnata) room
гостиница (gastínitsa) hotel
экскурсия (ekskúrsiya) excursion, tour

Instrumental: ко́мнатой (kómnatoi)
гости́ницей (gastínitsey)
экску́рсией (ekskúrsiyey)

The *Instrumental Case* is used mainly to denote the instrument of action or means *by* or *with which* a thing is done and the person performing the action. Very often a noun in the Instrumental Case corresponds with the English 'by' or 'with'.

This building was built by architect N.	Э́то зда́ние постро́ено архите́ктором Н.
	(Éto zdániye pastróyeno arkhityéktorom N.)
The excursion was conducted by guide M.	Экску́рсия была́ проведена́ экскурсово́дом М.
	(Ekskúrsiya builá pravyedyená ekskursovódom M.)
We open the door with a key.	Мы открыва́ем дверь ключо́м.
	(Mui atkruiváyem dvyér' klyuchóm.)

The *Instrumental Case* is used in sentences with the shortened adjective 'дово́лен/дово́льна/дово́льны' (davólyen/davól'na/davól'nui), content, satisfied.

We are satisfied/pleased with the service.	Мы дово́льны обслу́живанием.
	(Mui davól'nui apslúzhivaniyem.)
I did not like the excursion very much (I was not very satisfied with the excursion). (m.)	Я не о́чень дово́лен экску́рсией.
	(Ya nye óchen' davólyen ekskúrsiyey.)

For the use of the Instrumental Case with prepositions see PREPOSITIONS.

The *Prepositional Case*. This case is the easiest, because in this case the majority of nouns of all genders end with '-e' (-ye).

Nominative: f. ко́мната (kómnata) room
m. го́род (górot) town
n. письмо́ (pis'mó) letter

Prepositional:

(в) ко́мнате (f͡ kómnatye) (run them together)

(в) го́роде (f͡ górodye) (run them together)

(в) письме́ (f͡ pis'mýe) (run them together)

The *Prepositional Case* is always used with prepositions. The most important are: '**в**', '**на**', 'in', 'on'.

We are now staying *in* the Hotel 'Rossia'.	Мы живём сейча́с **в** гости́нице «Росси́я».
	(Mui zhivyóm seichás *v* gastínitsye 'Rassíya'.)
The 'Druzhba' shop is *on* Gorky Street.	Магази́н «Дру́жба» нахо́дится **на** у́лице Го́рького.
	(Magazín 'Drúzhba' nakhóditsya na úlitsye Gór'kavo.)

'**о**', '**об**', about: '**об**' is used when it precedes a word starting with a vowel.

Tell us about this district. Расскажи́те нам **об** э́том райо́не.

(Rasskazhítye nam *ob* étom rayónye.)

On the use of this case see IN/INTO.

Some foreign words in Russian are always used in one and the same form, i.e. they are not declinable. The main ones are:

бюро́	(byuró)	bureau, office
кафе́	(kafyé)	café, coffee-house
кино́	(kinó)	cinema
ко́фе	(kófye)	coffee
метро́	(myetró)	Metro, underground railway
пальто́	(pal'tó)	coat
такси́	(taksí)	taxi
шоссе́	(shassyé)	highway, motor road

Every, Everybody, Everything

every	m.	ка́ждый	(kázhduiy)
	f.	ка́ждая	(kázhdaya)
	n.	ка́ждое	(kázhdoye)
	pl.	ка́ждые	(kázhduiye)
everybody	m.	ка́ждый	(kázhduiy)
	pl.	все	(fsyé)
everything	n.	всё	(fsyó)

He goes to the cinema every day.	Он хо́дит в кино́ ка́ждый де́нь.
	(On khódit f kinó kázhduiy dyén'.)
Every street has its name.	Ка́ждая у́лица име́ет своё назва́ние.
	(Kázhdaya úlitsa imyéyet svayó nazvánie.)
Everyone is very satisfied.	Всё о́чень дово́льны.
	(Fsyé óchen' davól'nui.)
I understand everything you say.	Я понима́ю всё, что вы говори́те.
	(Ya panimáyu fsyó, shtó vui gavarítye.)

To Feel

Imperf. **Чу́вствовать** (chústvavat')
Present:

I feel	я чу́вствую	(ya chústvuyu)
you feel	вы чу́вствуете	(vui chústvuyetye)
he feels	он чу́вствует	(on chústvuyet)
we feel	мы чу́вствуем	(mui chústvuyem)
they feel	они́ чу́вствуют	(aní chústvuyut)

Past: m. чу́вствовал (chústvaval)
     f. чу́вствовала (chústvavala)
    pl. чу́вствовали (chústvavali)

Future: I shall feel я бу́ду чу́вствовать
                                (ya búdu chústvavat')
          you will feel вы бу́дете чу́вствовать
                                (vui búdyetye chústvavat')
          he will feel он бу́дет чу́вствовать
                                (on búdyet chústvavat')

Perf. **Почу́вствовать** (pachústvavat')
Future:

  I will feel   я почу́вствую   (ya pachústvuyu), etc.

Past:

  I felt   я почу́вствовал   (ya pachústvaval), etc.

How do you feel?	Ка́к вы себя́ чу́вствуете?
(*Literally*: How do you yourself feel?)	(Kák vui syebyá chústvuyetye?)
I feel well.	Я чу́вствую себя́ хорошо́.
	(Ya chústvuyu syebyá kharashó.)
We feel unwell (badly).	Мы пло́хо себя́ чу́вствуем.
	(Mui plókho syebyá chústvuyem.)

SPEAK, READ, WRITE RUSSIAN

Yesterday I stayed at home because I felt ill. (m.)
Вчера́ я оста́лся до́ма, потому́ что я пло́хо себя́ чу́вствовал.
(Fcherá ya astálsya dóma, patamú shto ya plókho syebyá chústvaval.)

If my wife feels unwell, we'll stay at home.
Е́сли моя́ жена́ бу́дет пло́хо себя́ чу́вствовать, мы оста́немся до́ма.
(Yésli mayá zhená búdyet plókho syebyá chústvavat', mui astányemsya dóma.)

Must, Ought, Should

Present:
- m. я/он до́лжен (ya/on dólzhen)
- f. я/она́ должна́ (ya/oná dalzhná)
- pl. мы/они́ должны́ (mui/aní dalzhnuí

Past:
- m. я/он был до́лжен (ya/on buil dólzhen)
- f. я/она́ была́ должна́ (ya/oná builá dalzhná)
- pl. мы/они́ бы́ли должны́ (mui/aní buíli dalzhnuí)

Future:
я бу́ду до́лжен/должна́ (ya búdu dólzhen/dalzhná)
вы бу́дете должны́ (vui búdyetye dalzhnuí)
он бу́дет до́лжен (on búdyet dólzhen)
она́ бу́дет должна́ (oná búdyet dolzhná)
мы бу́дем должны́ (mui búdyem dalzhnuí)
они́ бу́дут должны́ (aní búdut dalzhnuí)

I must go home.
Я до́лжен идти́ домо́й.
(Ya dólzhen ittí damói.)

MUST, OUGHT, SHOULD

You must be here tomorrow.	Вы должны́ быть здесь за́втра. (Vui dalzhnuí buit' zdyés' záftra.)
She should not do that.	Она́ не должна́ э́того де́лать. (Oná nye dalzhná étovo dyélat'.)
He should have done it long ago.	Он до́лжен был э́то сде́лать давно́. (On dólzhen buil éto zdyélat' davnó.)
You shouldn't have waited here.	Вы не должны́ бы́ли жда́ть здесь. (Vui nye dalzhnuí buíli zhdát' zdyés'.)
We shall have to send a telegram.	Мы должны́ бу́дем посла́ть телегра́мму. (Mui dalzhnuí búdyem poslát' tyelyegrámu.)

TO NEED

Need is expressed with the help of 'ну́жен' (núzhen), 'нужна́' (nuzhná) and 'нужны́' (nuzhnuí). These words agree with the noun in number and gender, e.g.:

I need a dictionary.	Мне ну́жен слова́рь. (Mnyé núzhen slavár'.)	m.
I need one stamp.	Мне нужна́ одна́ ма́рка. (Mnyé nuzhná adná márka.)	f.
I need some good records.	Мне нужны́ хоро́шие пласти́нки. (Mnyé nuzhnuí kharóshiye plastínki.)	pl.

137

The need of something is denoted by a noun or personal pronoun in the Dative (see CASES OF PRONOUNS).

We need one ticket.	Нам нýжен одúн билéт.
	(Nam núzhen adín bilyét.)
We need some new books.	Нам нужны́ нóвые кнúги.
	(Nam nuzhnuí nóvuiye knígi.)
Do you need these newspapers?	Вам нужны́ э́ти газéты?
	(Vam nuzhnuí éti gazyétui?)

Note the use of 'нýжно' (núzhno) with the infinitive, as follows:

I must ring up.	Мнé нýжно позвонúть по телефóну.
	(Mnyé núzhno pazvanít' po tyelyefónu.)
We must send a telegram.	Нам нýжно послáть телегрáмму.
	(Nam núzhno paslát' tyelyegrámu.)
What do you need to buy?	Что вам нýжно купúть?
	(Shtó vam núzhno kupít'?)

NEGATION

The negative 'не' (nye) is always placed before the word which is negated, e.g.

I can't do that.	Я не могý э́то сдéлать.
	(Ya nye magú éto zdyélat'.)
The shops are not open every day.	Магазúны рабóтают не кáждый дéнь.
(*Literally*: . . . do not work . . .)	(Magazínui rabótayut nye kázhduiy dyén'.)

NEGATION

It is not cold today.	Сегодня не холодно.
	(Syevódnya nye khóladno.)

Sometimes 'не' and the word it negates are joined in spelling:

That hat is not expensive.	Эта шапка недорогая.
	(Éta shápka nyedoragáya.)
I think that I am unwell.	Мне кажется, что я нездоров. (m.)
	(Mnye kázhetsya, shto ya nyezdaróf.

The negative 'нет' (nyet) can be used as a short form negative answer, e.g.:

Have you bought newspapers? No.	Вы купили газеты?—Нет.
	(Vui kupíli gazyétui?—Nyét.)

'Нет' can also correspond to the Present Tense of 'to have' or 'there is/there are' plus a negative.

I have no money.	У меня нет денег.
	(U myenyá nyét dyények.)
You have no tickets.	У вас нет билетов.
	(U vas nyét bilyétof.)
There is no mirror here.	Здесь нет зеркала.
	(Zdyés' nyét zyérkala.)
There are no flowers in the room.	В комнате нет цветов.
	(F kómnatye nyét tsvyetóf.)

For past and future, 'не' is used with 'быть', to be, in the 3rd person singular of the neuter gender.

I shall have no money tomorrow. (I shan't have any money tomorrow.)	У меня не будет денег завтра.
	(U myenyá nye búdyet dyények záftra.)

139

I had no money yesterday.	У меня́ не́ бы́ло де́нег вчера́. (U myenyá nyé buílo dyények fcherá.)
There will be no mirror here.	Здесь не бу́дет зе́ркала. (Zdyés' nye búdyet zyérkala.)
There was no mirror here.	Здесь не́ бы́ло зе́ркала. (Zdyés' nyé buílo zyérkala.)

Note the Genitive of the noun following a negative verb. Compare:

I have bought the newspapers.	Я купи́л газе́ты. (Ya kupíl gazyétui.)
I have not bought newspapers.	Я не́ купи́л газе́т. Gen. pl. (Ya nyé kupíl gazyét.)
There is a mirror here.	Здесь есть зе́ркало. (Zdyés' yést' zyérkalo.)
There was no mirror here.	Здесь не́ бы́ло зе́ркала. Gen. (Zdyés' nyé buílo zyérkala.)

The negatives 'не' and 'нет' can also be used in sentences already containing the negative pronouns and adverbs 'никто́' (niktó) and 'никого́' (nikavó), nobody, no-one; 'ничто́' (nishtó) and 'ничего́' (nichevó), nothing; 'никогда́' (nikogdá), never; and 'нигде́' (nigdyé), nowhere.

There is nobody here.	Здесь никого́ не́т. (Zdyés' nikavó nyét.)
I see nothing.	Я ничего́ не ви́жу. (Ya nichevó nye vízhu.)
I have never been to the Caucasus.	Я никогда́ не́ был на Кавка́зе. (Ya nikagdá nyé buíl na Kafkázye.)

NEGATION

We have not seen such good and inexpensive books anywhere.	Мы нигде́ не ви́дели таки́х хоро́ших и дешёвых кни́г. (Mui nigdyé nye vídyeli takíkh kharóshikh i dyeshóvikh kníg.)

The negative often affects the aspect of the verb. The imperfective verb often becomes the preferable, if not the only possible form to use after a negative, e.g.:

I want to answer you.	Я хочу́ отве́тить вам. (Perf.) (Ya khachú atvyétit' vam.)
I do not want to answer you.	Я не хочу́ отвеча́ть вам. (Imperf.) (Ya nye khachú atvyechát' vam.)
Read this book.	Прочита́йте э́ту кни́гу. (Perf.) (Prachitáytye étu knígu.)
Don't read this book.	Не чита́йте э́ту кни́гу. (Imperf.) (Nye chitáytye étu knígu.)

NUMERALS

1 оди́н m. (adín)
  одна́ f. (adná)
  одно́ n. (adnó)
2 два m. (dva)
  две f. (dvye)
3 три (tri)
4 четы́ре (chyetuírye)
5 пять (pyat')
6 шесть (shyest')
7 семь (syem')
8 во́семь (vósyem')
9 де́вять (dyévyat')
10 де́сять (dyésyat')
11 оди́ннадцать (adínnattsat')
12 двена́дцать (dvyenáttsat')

13	тринáдцать (trináttsat')	28	двáдцать вóсемь
14	четы́рнадцать (chyetuírnattsat')	29	двáдцать дéвять
15	пятнáдцать (pyatnáttsat')	30	три́дцать (tríttsat')
16	шестнáдцать (shyestnáttsat')	40	сóрок (sórok)
17	семнáдцать (syemnáttsat')	50	пятьдеся́т (pyat'desyát)
18	восемнáдцать (vosyemnáttsat')	60	шестьдеся́т (shyest'desyát)
19	девятнáдцать (dyevyatnáttsat')	70	сéмьдесят (syém'desyat)
20	двáдцать (dváttsat')	80	вóсемьдесят (vósyem'desyat)
21	двáдцать оди́н m. двáдцать однá f. двáдцать однó n.	90	девянóсто (dyevyanósto)
		100	сто (sto)
		200	двéсти (dvyésti)
		300	три́ста (trísta)
22	двáдцать два m. двáдцать две f.	400	четы́реста (chyetuíryesta)
23	двáдцать три	500	пятьсóт (pyat'sót)
24	двáдцать четы́ре	600	шестьсóт (shyest'sót)
25	двáдцать пять	700	семьсóт (syem'sót)
26	двáдцать шесть	800	восемьсóт (vosyem'sót)
27	двáдцать семь	900	девятьсóт (dyevyat'sót)

1,000	ты́сяча (tuísyacha)
3,000	три ты́сячи (tri tuísyachi)
5,000	пять ты́сяч (pyat' tuísyach)
1,000,000	миллиóн (millión)
2,000,000	два миллиóна (dva millióna)
6,000,000	шесть миллиóнов (shest' milliónof)

один киломéтр (adín kilómyetr), one kilometre
однá минýта (adná minúta), one minute
однó окнó (adnó aknó), one window

два киломéтра (dva kilómyetra), two kilometres
две минýты (dvye minútui), two minutes
два окнá (dva akná), two windows

дéсять киломéтров (dyésyat' kilómyetrof), ten kilometres
дéсять минýт (dyésyat' minút), ten minutes
дéсять окóн (dyésyat' akón), ten windows
одúн рýбль, однá копéйка (adín rúbl', adná kapyéyka),
   1 rouble, 1 copek
два рубля́, две копéйки (dva rublyá, dvye kapyéyki),
   2 roubles, 2 copeks
пятьдеся́т рублéй, пятьдеся́т копéек (pyat'desyát rublyéy,
   pyatdyesyát kapyéyek), 50 roubles, 50 copeks

Ordinal Numbers

Russian ordinal numbers are adjectives, and so must agree with the nouns that follow them: пéрвый день (pyérvuiy dyen'), first day; пéрвая поéздка (pyérvaya payéstka), first journey; пéрвое слóво (pyérvoye slóvo), first word.

Ordinal numbers from 1st to 10th:

пéрвый, пéрвая, пéрвое	(pyérvuiy, pyérvaya, pyérvoye)
вторóй, втора́я, второ́е	(ftarói, ftaráya, ftaróye)
трéтий, трéтья, трéтье	(tryétiy, tryét'ya, tryét'ye)
четвёртый, четвёртая, четвёртое	(chyetvyórtui, chyetvyórtaya, chyetvyórtoye)

пя́тый, пя́тая, пя́тое	(pyátuiy, pyátaya, pyátoye)
шесто́й, шеста́я, шесто́е	(shyestói, shyestáya, shyestóye)
седьмо́й, седьма́я, седьмо́е	(syed'mói, syed'máya, syed'móye)
восмьо́й, восьма́я, вомсьо́е	(vas'mói, vas'máya, vas'móye)
девя́тый, девя́тая, девя́тое	dyevyátuiy, dyevyátaya, dyevyátoye)
деся́тый, деся́тая, деся́тое	(dyesyátuiy, dyesyátaya, dyesyátoye)

Most ordinal numbers after the first ten are formed by adding '-ый', '-ая', '-ое' to the last consonant of the corresponding cardinal numerals: 'оди́ннадцать—оди́ннадцатый', 'трина́дцать—трина́дцатый' (eleven—11th, thirteen—13th).

Ordinal numbers are less common than cardinal numbers.

1. *Denoting centuries*:

the nineteenth century	девятна́дцатый век (dyevyatnáttsatuiy vyek)
In the twentieth century	в двадца́том ве́ке (v dvattsátom vyékye)

2. *Usage with buses, trolleybuses, etc.*:

Trolleybus No. 33	три́дцать тре́тий тролле́йбус (tríttsat' tryétiy trallyéybus) or тролле́йбус но́мер три́дцать три (trallyéybus nómyer tríttsat' tri)

NUMERALS

Bus No. 40
    сороковóй автóбус
    (sorokavói áftobus)
    or автóбус нóмер сóрок
    (aftóbus ņómyer sórok)

3. *Telling the time*:

(It is) half past one
    Половúна вторóго
    (Palavína ftaróvo)
    or Одúн час трúдцать минýт
    (Adín chas tríttsat' minút)

Ten past two
    Дéсять минýт трéтьего
    (Dyésyat' minut tryét'yevo)
    or
    Два часá дéсять минýт
    (Dva chasá dyésyat' minút)

(See ORDINAL NUMBERS.)

ONE—THEY

Idiomatic expressions:

People say, do
They say, do } говорят, делают
One says, does } (gavaryát, dyélayut)
It's said, done

They say you are leaving tomorrow.
    Говорят, что вы завтра уезжáете.
    (Gavaryát, shto vui záftra uyezháyetye.)

They were giving the weather forecast on the radio.
    По рáдио передавáли свóдку погóды.
    (Po rádio pyeryedaváli svótku pagódui.)

Popular usage with the words 'мо́жно' (mózhno), one may, one can; 'нельзя́' (nyel'zyá), one must not; 'ну́жно' (núzhno), one must, one wants, needs:

May one smoke here? — Здесь мо́жно кури́ть? (Zdyes' mózhno kurít'?)

How can one do that? — Ка́к э́то мо́жно сде́лать? (Kák éto mózhno zdyélat'?)

One must answer this letter. (This letter must be answered.) — Ну́жно отве́тить на э́то письмо́. (Núzhno atvyétit' na éto pis'mó.)

One must not park here. (*Literally*: ... place the car here.) — Здесь нельзя́ ста́вить маши́ну. (Zdyés' nyel'zyá stávit' mashínu.)

What does one answer to 'Bon Appetit!'? (*Literally*: What should one say if they say ...) — Что́ ну́жно сказа́ть, е́сли говоря́т «Прия́тного аппети́та»? (Shtó núzhno skazát', yésli gavaryát 'Priyátnavo appyetíta'?)

To Pay

Imperf. **Плати́ть** (platít')
Present:

I pay	я плачу́	(ya plachú)
you pay	вы пла́тите	(vui plátitye)
he pays	он пла́тит	(on plátit)
we pay	мы плати́м	(mui platím)
they pay	они́ пла́тят	(aní plátyat)

146

TO PAY

Perf. Заплати́ть (zaplatít')
Future:
I will pay	я заплачу́	(ya zaplachú)
you will pay	вы запла́тите	(vui zaplátitye)
they will pay	они́ запла́тят	(aní zplátyat)

Past:
I/he paid	я/он заплати́л m.	
	(ya/on zaplatíl)	
I/she paid	я/она́ заплати́ла f.	
	(ya/oná zaplatíla)	
we/they paid	мы/они́ заплати́ли pl.	
	(mui/aní zaplatíli)	

Imperative: Pay (please) Плати́те (Platítye)
                         Заплати́те (Zaplatítye)
         Don't pay Не плати́те (Nye platítye)

Do you pay in roubles or in pounds?	Вы пла́тите рубля́ми и́ли фу́нтами?
	(Vui plátitye rublyámi íli fúntami?)
We are paying with pounds.	Мы пла́тим фу́нтами.
	(Mui platím fúntami.)
I shall pay tomorrow.	Я заплачу́ за́втра.
	(Ya zaplachú záftra.)
Please pay the money at the cash-desk.	Плати́те де́ньги в ка́ссу.
	(Platítye dyén'gi f kássu.)
I have paid (f.) already. Here is the bill.	Я уже́ заплати́ла. Вот чек.
	(Ya uzhé zaplatíla. Vót chék.)

The Russian word 'чек' (chek) can also mean' a cheque'.

How much must I (m.) pay the doctor?	Ско́лько я до́лжен заплати́ть врачу́?
	(Skól'ko ya dólzhen zaplatít' vrachú?)

You don't have to pay anything.	Вы ничего́ не должны́ плати́ть.
	(Vui nichyevó nye dalzhnuí platít'.)

MEETING PEOPLE

In Russian it is common practice and polite to address people who are neither members of the family nor close friends by their Christian name and patronymic, e.g. Boris Alexandrovich Ivanov you would address as Boris Alexandrovich, namely, Boris, son of Alexander. It is quite possible to meet and speak with Boris Alexandrovich many times and never know his surname. In general practice among Russians a courtesy title equivalent to the English 'Mister' is never used, but may be used when speaking to an Englishman. See p. 150.

Good morning.	До́брое у́тро.
	(Dóbroye útro.)
Good day.	До́брый де́нь.
	(Dóbruiy dyén'.)
Good evening.	До́брый ве́чер.
	(Dóbruiy vyéchyer.)
How do you do?	Здра́вствуйте?
	(Zdrástvuytye?)
How are things?	Ка́к ва́ши дела́?
	(Kák váshi dyelá?)
Very happy/pleased to make your acquaintance.	О́чень рад познако́миться.
	(Óchen' rat paznakómit'sya.)
Where do you come from?	Отку́да вы?
(*Literally*: From where are you?)	(Atkúda vui?)

MEETING PEOPLE

What country are you from?	Из какóй вы страны́? (Iz kakói vui stranuí?)
I (come) from England.	Я из А́нглии. (Ya iz Ánglii.)
We (come) from Canada.	Мы из Канáды. (Mui iz Kanádui.)
When did you arrive?	Когдá вы приéхали? (Kagdá vui priyékhali?)
We arrived two days ago.	Мы приéхали двá дня́ назáд. (Mui priyékhali dvá dnyá nazát.)
Where have you already been?	Гдé вы ужé побывáли? (Gdyé vui uzhé pabuiváli?)
We have been to Moscow and to Leningrad.	Мы бы́ли в Москвé и в Ленингрáде. (Mui buíli v Maskvyé i v Lyeningrádye.).
Do you like our town?	Вам нрáвится наш гóрод? (Vam nrávitsya nash górot?)
Where do you want to go?	Кудá вы хотúте поéхать? (Kudá vui khatítye payékhat'?)
What do you want to see?	Чтó вы хотúте посмотрéть? (Shtó vui khatítye pasmatryét'?)
Do come here again.	Приезжáйте к нáм ещё рáз. (Priyezháytye k nam yeshchó ráz.)
Goodbye.	Дó свидáния. (Dá-svidániya.)

SPEAK, READ, WRITE RUSSIAN

Well (not too well).	Хорошо́ (не о́чень хорошо́). (Kharashó (nye óchen' kharashó).)
May (I) come in?	Мо́жно войти́? (Mózhno vaytí?)
Come in, please.	Входи́те, пожа́луйста. (Fkhadítye, pazháluysta.)
Take a seat.	Сади́тесь. (Sadítyes'.)
Do you smoke?	Вы ку́рите? (Vui kúritye?)
Another cigarette?	Ещё сигаре́ту? (Yeshchó sigaryétu?)
Michael, I want to introduce you.	Ма́йкл, я хочу́ предста́вить тебя́. (Máykl, ya khachú pretstávit' tyebyá.)
Ivan Sergeyevich, let me introduce Mr. Morris to you.	Ива́н Серге́евич, разреши́те предста́вить вам ми́стера Мо́рриса. (Iván Syergéyevich, razryeshítye pryetstávit' vam místyera Mórrisa.)
This is Mr. Morris and this is Mr. Jones.	Э́то ми́стер Мо́ррис, а э́то ми́стер Джо́нс. (Éto místyer Mórris, a éto místyer Dzhóns.)
Let me introduce myself. My (sur)name is Morozov.	Разреши́те предста́виться. Моя́ фами́лия Моро́зов. (Razryeshítye pryetstávit'sya. Mayá famíliya Marózof.)

MEETING PEOPLE

What is your name?	Как вас зовут?
	(Kák vas zavút?)
My name is Nikolai Petrovich.	Меня зовут Николай Петрович.
	(Myenyá zavút Nikalái Pyetróvich.)

Money Matters

We have some money.	У нас есть деньги.
	(U nas yést' dyén'gi.)
I have little money.	У меня мало денег.
	(U myenyá málo dyények.)
Have you no money?	У вас нет денег?
	(U vas nyét dyények?)
I want to change some English money for roubles.	Я хочу обменять английские деньги на рубли.
	(Ya khachú abmyenyát' anglíyskiye dyén'gi na rublí.)
Where is the bank?	Где находится банк?
	(Gdyé nakhóditsya bánk?)
Can I change traveller's cheques?	Можно обменять дорожные чеки?
	(Mózhno obmyenyát' darózhnuiye chéki?)
How much do you want?	Сколько вы хотите?
	(Skól'ko vui khatítye?)
Give me one hundred roubles.	Дайте мне сто рублей.
	(Dáytye mnyé stó rublyéy.)
What is the rate of exchange now?	Каков сейчас курс?
	(Kakóf seichás kúrs?)
Sign here, please.	Пожалуйста, распишитесь здесь.
	(Pazháluysta, raspishítyes' zdyés'.)

SPEAK, READ, WRITE RUSSIAN

| Here is your money, sir. (*Literally*: ... please.) | Вот ваши деньги, пожалуйста. (Vót váshi dyén'gi, pazháluysta.) |

USE OF 'ABOUT'

Approximately: около (ókolo)
    Concerning: о, об (o) (ob); see page 133.

The train leaves at about ten.	Поезд уходит **около** десяти часов. (Póyest ukhódit *ókolo* dyesyatí chasóf.)
Now it is about 8 a.m.	Сейчас **около** восьми часов утра. (Seichás *ókolo* vas'mí chasóf útra.)
We are speaking about our trip.	Мы говорим **о** нашей поездке. (Mui gavarím *o* náshei payéstkye.)
Tell me about your work.	Расскажите мне **о** вашей работе. (Rasskazhítye mnyé *o* vashéi rabótye.)
What are you thinking about?	**О** чём вы думаете? (*O* chóm vui dúmayetye?)
I have heard about it.	Я слышал **об** этом. (Ya sluíshal *ob* étom.)

The preposition 'o', 'об' requires the Prepositional Case,

152

USE OF 'ABOUT'

while 'около' requires the Genitive Case. (See PREPOSITIONS.)

PREPOSITIONS

Every Russian preposition involves a certain case of the noun.

Prepositions governing the *Genitive*:

1. '**без**' (byez, byes), without.

Give me coffee without milk.	Дайте кофе **без** молока.
	(Dáytye kófye *byez* malaká.)
I wanted (m.) tea without sugar.	Я хотел чай **без** сахара.
	(Ya khatyél chái *byes* sákhara.)

2. '**для**' (dlya), for, to.

I need stamps for a letter to England.	Мне нужны марки **для** письма в Англию.
	(Mnyé nuzhnuí márki *dlya* pis'má v Ángliyu.)
I shall do it for you.	Я сделаю это **для** вас.
	(Ya zdyélayu éto *dlya* vás.)

3. '**до**' (do, da), to.

How does one get to the Exhibition?	Как доехать **до** выставки?
	(Kák dayékhat' *do* vuístafki?)
Is it far to the airport? (*Literally*: Tell (me), etc. . . . .)	Скажите, **до** аэропорта далеко?
	(Skazhítye, *da* aeropórta dalyekó?)
It is ten kilometres to the airport.	**До** аэропорта десять километров.
	(*Da* aeropórta dyésyat' kilomyétrof.)

153

4. **'около'** (ókolo), about, near.

It is now about five o'clock.	Сейча́с **о́коло** пяти́ часо́в.
	(Seichás *ókolo* pyatí chasóv.)
The post office is near the hotel.	По́чта нахо́дится **о́коло** го́стиницы.
	(Póchta nakhóditsya *ókolo* gastínitsui.)

5. **'от'** (ot), from.

Zagorsk is not far from Moscow.	Заго́рск нахо́дится недалеко́ **от** Москвы́.
	(Zagórsk nakhóditsya nyedalyekó *ot* Maskvuí.)
We live a long way from Red Square.	Мы живём далеко́ **от** Кра́сной пло́щади.
	(Mui zhivyóm dalyekó *ot* Krasnói plóshchadi.)
It is 8,000 kilometres from Moscow to Vladivostok.	**От** Москвы́ до Владивосто́ка во́семь ты́сяч киломе́тров.
	(*Ot* Maskvuí da Vladivastóka vósyem' tuísyach kilomyétrof.)

6. **'из'** (iz, is), from.

From what country are you?	Из како́й вы страны́?
	(*Iz* kakói vui stranuí?)
We are from England.	Мы **из** А́нглии.
	(Mui *iz* Ánglii.)
I am from Canada.	Я **из** Кана́ды.
	(Yá *is* Kanádui.)
We are from the U.S.A.	Мы **из** США.
	(Mui *iz* ÉsShá-Á.)

PREPOSITIONS

7. **'с ... до'** (s ... do/da), from ... to (till).

| The shop is open from 0800 till 2100 hours. | Магазин работает **с** восьми **до** двадцати одного часа. (Magazín rabótayet *s* vas'mí *da* dvattsatí adnavó chasá.) |

8. **'у'** (u)—in phrases of possession.

| I have the ticket already. | У меня уже есть билет. (*U* myenyá uzhé yést' bilyét.) |
| The tourists have a very interesting programme. | У туристов очень интересная программа. (*U* turístof óchen' intyeryésnaya pragrámma.) |

Prepositions governing the *Accusative*:

1. **'в'** and **'на'** (v and na) (when denoting direction), to.

| Today we are going to the theatre. | Сегодня мы идём **в** театр. (Syevódnya mui idyóm *f* teátr.) |
| I want to go to the Exhibition. | Я хочу поехать **на** Выставку. (Ya khachú payékhat' *na* Vuístafku.) |

2. **'в'** (when denoting time), at, on.

| We shall come on Thursday. | Мы приедем **в** четверг. (Mui priyédyem *f* chyetvyérk.) |
| I am leaving on Friday. | Я уезжаю **в** пятницу. (Ya uyezháyu *f* pyátnitsu.) |

3. **'через'** (chéryes), in, through.

| In an hour. | **Через** час. (*Chéryes* chas.) |

In a week.	Через неделю.
	(*Chéryes* nyedyélyu.)

Preposition governing the *Dative*:
'с' (s), with.

Give me black coffee with sugar.	Дайте чёрный кофе **с** сахаром.
	(Dáytye chórnuiy kófye *s* sákharom.)
I came with (my) wife.	Я приехал **с** женой.
	(Ya priyékhal *s* zhenói.)

Prepositions governing the *Prepositional*:

1. **'в'**, **'на'** (v, na) (when indicating location), on, at.

The 'Souvenirs' shop is on Gorky Street.	Магазин «Сувениры» находится **на** улице Горького.
	(Magazín 'Suvyenírui' nakhóditsya *na* úlitsye Gór'kavo.)
We stay at the 'Rossia' hotel.	Мы живём **в** гостинице «Россия».
	(Mui zhivyóm *v* gastínitsye 'Rassíya'.)
One can buy postcards in a post office.	Почтовые открытки можно купить **на** почте.
	(Pachtóvuiye atkruítki mózhno kupít' na póchtye.)

2. **'в'** (v), in, during—with the names of the months.

We were in Sochi in September.	Мы были **в** Сочи **в** сентябре.
	(Mui buíli f Sóchi f syentyabryé.)

PREPOSITIONS

I want to go to Kiev in May.	Я хочу́ пое́хать в Ки́ев в ма́е. (Ya khachú payékhat' f Kíyef *v* máye.)

3. **'о', 'об'** (o, ob), about, concerning.

Tell us about your work.	Расскажи́те о ва́шей рабо́те. (Rasskazhítye *o* váshyey rabótye.)
I will tell (you) about this museum.	Я расскажу́ об э́том музе́е. (Ya rasskazhú *ab* étom muzyéye.)

See also USE OF 'ABOUT' and page 133.

IN, INTO, TO

Any of these prepositions can correspond to **'в'** (v, f) and **'на'** (na) in Russian.

When referring to motion (where to?) these prepositions are followed by the *Accusative*, e.g.:

Tomorrow we shall go to Leningrad.	За́втра мы е́дем в Ленингра́д. (Acc.) (Záftra mui yédyem v Lyeningrát.)
We want to go to the Tolstoy Museum.	Мы хоти́м пойти́ в музе́й Толсто́го. (Acc.) (Mui khatím páyti v muzyéy Talstóvo.)
I want to go to Red Square.	Я хочу́ пое́хать на Кра́сную пло́щадь. (Acc.) (Ya khachú payékhat' na Krásnuyu plóshchat'.)

In referring to the place where the thing is (or where something is being done to it), the *Prepositional* Case is used:

We were in Leningrad in the winter.	Мы бы́ли в Ленингра́де зимо́й. (Prep.) (Mui buíli v Lyeningrádye zimói.)
I saw (m.) this portrait in the Tolstoy Museum.	Я ви́дел э́тот портре́т в музе́е Толсто́го. (Prep.) (Ya vídyel étot partryét v Muzyéye Talstóvo.)
The Kremlin is in Red Square.	Кре́мль нахо́дится на Кра́сной пло́щади. (Prep.) (Kryéml' nakhóditsya na Krásnoi plóshchadi.)
In England it is summer now.	В А́нглии сейча́с ле́то. (V Ánglii seichás lyéto.)
When were you in France?	Когда́ вы бы́ли во Фра́нции? (Kagdá vui buíli vo Frántsii?)
I was in France in the summer. (m.)	Я был во Фра́нции ле́том. (Ya buíl vo Frántsii lyétom.)

To give the date use an ordinal number of the neuter gender (see NUMERALS) plus the name of the month in the *Genitive*, e.g.:

What is today's date?	Како́е сего́дня число́? (Kakóye syevódnya chisló?)
Today is the third of May/September.	Сего́дня тре́тье ма́я/сентября́. (Syevódnya tryét'ye máya/syentyabryá.)

THE PASSIVE VOICE

Passive constructions are far less common in Russian than in English, and they are hardly ever used in colloquial speech. Compare:

THE PASSIVE VOICE

Nothing can be done.	Ничего нельзя сделать.
	(Nichevó nyel'zyá zdyélat'.)
What were you told?	Что вам сказали?
	(Shtó vam skazáli?)
I was given a (fountain) pen and a pencil.	Мне дали ручку и карандаш.
	(Mnyé dáli rúchku i karandásh.)

An English phrase in the Passive can be translated by a reflexive ending, '-ся', '-сь', or by 'быть' (buit'), to be, plus a short-form passive participle.

The house is being built.	Дом строится.
	(Dom stróitsya.)
The house was being built.	Дом строился.
	(Dom stroílsya.)
A house will be built here.	Здесь будет строится дом.
	(Zdyés' búdyet stróitsya dóm.)
The house is built.	Дом построен.
	(Dóm pastróyen.)
The house was built long ago.	Дом был построен давно.
	(Dóm buil pastróyen davnó.)
The house will be built quickly.	Дом будет построен быстро.
	(Dóm búdyet pastróyen buístro.)

To Write

Imperf. **Писать** (pisát')
Present:

I write	я пишу	(ya pishú)
you write	вы пишете	(vui píshetye)

SPEAK, READ, WRITE RUSSIAN

he writes	он пи́шет	(on píshet)
we write	мы пи́шем	(mui píshem)
they write	они́ пи́шут	(aní píshut)

Perf.: **Написа́ть** (napisát')
Future:

I will write	я напишу́	(ya napishú)
you will write	вы напи́шете	(vui napíshetye)
he will write	он напи́шет	(on napíshet)
we will write	мы напи́шем	(mui napíshem)
they will write	они́ напи́шут	(aní napíshut)

Past:

I/he wrote	я/он написа́л	(ya/on napisál) m.
I/she wrote	я/она́ написа́ла	(ya/oná napisála) f.
we/they wrote	мы/они́ написа́ли	(mui/aní napisáli) pl.

Imperative: Imperf.: Write! Пиши́те! (Pishítye!)
           Perf.: Write! Напиши́те! (Napishítye!)

What are you writing?	Что́ вы пи́шите?
	(Shtó vui píshitye?)
I am writing a letter home.	Я пишу́ письмо́ домо́й.
	(Ya pishú pis'mó damói.)
I have already written (f.) the letter.	Я уже́ написа́ла письмо́.
	(Ya uzhé napisála pis'mó.)
Write us (a letter). Here is our address.	Напиши́те нам. Во́т на́ш а́дрес.
	(Napishítye nam. Vót nash ádryes.)
Write to me in Russian.	Пиши́те мне́ по-ру́сски.
	(Pishítye mnyé pa-rússki.)